Wow! Smart Vocabulary

5

집필진: 김미희, E-NEXT 영어연구회

김미희, 박경희, 박소현, 임지연, 홍정민, 한성욱, Christina KyungJin Ham, Leeanne Madden(Editorial Advisor)

김미희 선생님은 이화여자대학교 영어교육과를 졸업하고 EBS English에서 방영하는 'Yo! Yo! Play Time'과 'EBS 방과 후 영어'를 집필 및 검토하셨으며, 베스트셀러인 '10시간 영문법'과 '영어 글쓰기왕 비법 따라잡기' 등의 많은 영어교재를 집필하셨습니다. E-NEXT 영어연구회는 김미희 선생님을 중심으로, 세계 영어교육의 흐름에 발맞추어 효과적이고 바람직한 영어 교수·학습 방법을 연구하는 영어교육 전문가들의 모임입니다.

Smart Vocabulary 5

지은이 김미희
펴낸이 정규도
펴낸곳 다락원

초판 1쇄 발행 2011년 12월 5일
초판 5쇄 발행 2024년 7월 3일

편집 최주연, 장경희, 오승현
영문교정 Michael A. Putlack
디자인 정현석, 윤미주, 김은미, 정규옥

다락원 경기도 파주시 문발로 211
전화: (02)736-2031 내선 251~252
Fax: (02)732-2037
출판등록 1977년 9월 16일 제406-2008-000007호

값 9,500원

ISBN 978-89-277-4029-2
      978-89-277-4030-8(set)

http://www.darakwon.co.kr
다락원 홈페이지를 통해 책 속의 영문 해석 자료,
표제어 및 스토리 MP3 파일을 받아 보실 수 있습니다.

출간에 도움 주신 분들

신가윤(Brown International School 국제학교 분당캠퍼스 원장)
배정연(키다리교육센터 메인 강사)
Jeniffer Kim(English Hunters 원장)
전남숙(KidsCollege 원장)
Leigh Stella Lage(성남외국어고등학교 원어민교사)
조은정(아이스펀지 잉글리쉬 원감)
심희선 이영란 박종희
이선옥(OK's Class 원장)
박혜정(잉글루 고창 어학원 원장)

내지일러스트 강선용   **표지일러스트** 노유이

WOW! Smart Vocabulary를 추천합니다!

단어 공부는 외국어 공부의 기본이자 실력입니다. 단어 공부에 대한 의견이 분분하지만, 영어를 제 2외국어로 삼고 있는 우리 어린이들에게 단어 학습이 필요하다는 사실은 부정할 수 없습니다. 문제는 방법이지요. 단어의 철자와 뜻만 외우는 것은 너무 단편적이어서 큰 의미가 없습니다. 어린이들이 쉽고 재미있게 단어를 익히면서 실생활에서 활용할 수 있는 효과적인 단어 학습 방법이 필요합니다. 그런 의미에서, 기계적인 암기에서 끝나지 않고 꼭 필요한 단어들을 이야기 속에서 익힐 수 있는 WOW! Smart Vocabulary 시리즈를 적극 추천합니다.

김정렬 (한국교원대학교 영어교육과 교수, 초등영어교과서 저자, 한국초등영어교육학회 회장)

제시된 단어를 문제 풀이를 통해 이해 수준을 확인하던 기존의 어휘 학습 방법을 탈피하여, 학습자가 관심을 가질 수 있는 다양한 주제의 어휘들을 논픽션과 픽션으로 이루어진 스토리와 연계해서 자연스럽게 학습할 수 있는 점이 WOW! Smart Vocabulary 시리즈의 가장 큰 특징이라고 할 수 있습니다. 또한 워크북은 배운 단어들을 스스로 정리하고 확실히 익히는 데 매우 효과적인 문제 유형들로 이루어져 있네요.

샤이니 김재영 (EBS English 영어방송진행자)

단어를 많이 아는 것도 중요하지만 실제 생활에서 상황에 맞는 단어를 활용하는 것이 더욱 중요합니다. 같은 단어라 할지라도 때론 문장 속에서 여러 의미로 해석되기도 하고, 다른 뜻으로 쓰여지기도 합니다. WOW! Smart Vocabulary 시리즈는 초등학교에서 중학교까지 단계적으로 단어를 학습할 수 있도록 구성되어 있으며, 스토리 속에서 살아 움직이는 단어를 익혀 실제 생활에 활용할 수 있도록 전략적으로 구성되어 있어 재미와 지식, 단어의 실제적 활용을 동시에 잡는 단어 교재라고 여겨집니다.

조은옥 (성지초등학교 교감, 초등영어교과서 저자)

한 주제별로 논픽션, 픽션의 두 가지 레슨이 짝으로 이루어진 점이 아주 신선하네요. 또한 스토리 속에 학습 단어들을 적용해 가며 나의 단어를 만들어 갈 수 있게 해주는 구성도 마음에 듭니다. Unit마다 쉬운 단어부터 난이도 있는 단어 학습까지 할 수 있어서 학습자가 성취감을 느낌과 동시에 난이도 있는 단어에도 도전 정신을 갖도록 해주는 것이 이 책의 큰 매력입니다.

이수진 (코너스톤 국제학교 아카데믹매니저)

WOW! Smart Vocabulary 시리즈는 초등학교뿐 아니라 중학교 수준의 필수 어휘까지 주제에 맞게 학습할 수 있습니다. 단순히 뜻을 외우거나 어휘의 기능에만 초점을 두는 학습이 아니라 어휘의 문법적인 쓰임과 실용적인 표현을 통한 문장 활용까지 배울 수 있게 구성한 것이 좋습니다. 더 나아가 스토리 속에서 어휘를 익힘으로써 어휘 교재이면서도 어휘 수준을 능가하는 의미 있는 학습을 제공한다는 점이 큰 장점이라고 할 수 있습니다. 또한 효율적인 연습 문제 유형들도 돋보입니다.

박진희 (중탑초등학교 교사)

WOW! Smart Vocabulary has various nonfiction and fiction stories which give this book its charm. These interesting stories will keep students motivated. Along with engaging exercises, students are sure to efficiently learn new words from this book.

Janet Y Ko (용마초등학교 원어민 교사)

이 책의 구성과 특징

WOW! Smart Vocabulary에는 여러 영어 교육 전문가 선생님들이
오랜 시간 동안 현장에서 직접 적용해보고 지도해본 실제 경험이 고스란히 녹아 들어가 있습니다.
모든 Unit은 하나의 주제 아래 Nonfiction과 Fiction이라는
두 개의 쌍둥이 Lesson으로 이루어져 있습니다.
첫 번째 Lesson에서는 실화, 신문기사, 광고 등과 같이
사실적인 정보를 주는 이야기(Nonfiction)를 통해 단어들을 익힙니다.
두 번째 Lesson에서는 주인공과 함께 친구가 되어
가상의 이야기(Fiction) 속에 빠져들면서 단어를 배우게 됩니다.

표제어

주제에 따라 서로 연관성이 있는 표제어들을 제시하기 때문에 기억하기 쉽습니다. 사진이나 삽화를 통해 각 단어의 분명한 의미를 바로 파악할 수 있고, 시각적 연상을 통해 단어를 감각적으로 기억할 수 있습니다.

※ 단어 선정과 분류는 교과부 개정교육과정 기본어휘 목록표를 바탕으로 했으며, 이 외에도 실제 초등학생의 일상생활에서 친숙한 단어와 중학 영어 학습을 위해 꼭 알아두어야 할 단어까지 함께 제시했습니다.

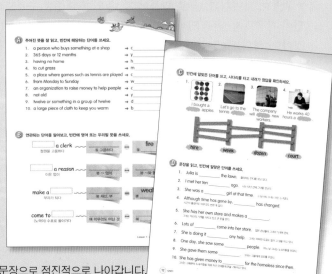

단계적인 연습문제

단계적인 연습문제 풀이를 통해 단어에서 구로, 구에서 문장으로 점진적으로 나아갑니다.
학습하는 단어와 관련하여 기억하기 쉽게 도와주는 확장형 연상문제도 있습니다.
단어의 철자만 익히는 것이 아니라, 그 단어가 문장 속에서 어떻게 쓰이는지 학습할 수 있습니다.

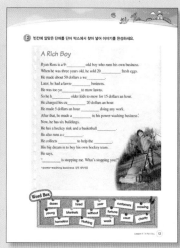

스토리 구성하기

각 Lesson의 마지막 단계는 Lesson에서 제시하는 학습단어들로
스토리를 만드는 것입니다. 논픽션과 픽션의 재미있는 쌍둥이 스토리 속에
녹아 있는 학습단어를 찾아 쓰면서, 배운 단어들이 실제 스토리 속에서
어떻게 살아 움직이는지 경험해 봅니다.

별책부록 - 워크북

본 책의 각 Unit에서 배운 학습단어의 우리말 뜻을 써 보며 스스로 실력을 체크하고,
각 Lesson마다 등장하는 스토리 속 문장을 통해 다시 한번 학습단어를 점검합니다.
이어지는 Review Test에서는 단어의 단순 암기가 아닌 실용적인 활용에 중점을 두고 구성한
다양한 유형의 문제들을 풀어보면서 실력을 확인해 봅니다.

학습 예시

WOW! Smart Vocabulary는 총 5권으로 구성되어 있고,
권 당 10개의 Unit, 한 Unit에 두 개의 Lesson이 들어있습니다.
한 Lesson을 학습하는 데 약 한 시간이 걸리므로,
한 Unit을 대체로 두 시간 동안 학습할 수 있습니다.
WOW! Smart Vocabulary를 일주일에 5시간 학습할 경우
권 당 4주, 총 5개월 정도가 소요됩니다.

	학습 시간	Unit / Lesson	표제어 수 & 비율	Total
1권	20시간 Lesson 당 1시간	10/20	Unit별 20개(Lesson별 10개) 교육부 제시 초등 기본어휘 70~80% / 중등 기본어휘 + 확장어휘 20~30%	200
2권	20시간 Lesson 당 1시간	10/20	Unit별 20개(Lesson별 10개) 교육부 제시 초등 기본어휘 60~70% / 중등 기본어휘 + 확장어휘 30~40%	200
3권	20시간 Lesson 당 1시간	10/20	Unit별 24개(Lesson별 12개) 교육부 제시 초등 기본어휘 50~60% / 중등 기본어휘 + 확장어휘 40~50%	240
4권	20시간 Lesson 당 1시간	10/20	Unit별 24개(Lesson별 12개) 교육부 제시 초등 기본어휘 40~50% / 중등 기본어휘 + 확장어휘 50~60%	240
5권	20시간 Lesson 당 1시간	10/20	Unit별 28개(Lesson별 14개) 교육부 제시 초등 기본어휘 30~40% / 중등 기본어휘 + 확장어휘 60~70%	280
총 학습단어 수				1,160

5권 단어구성표

5권		초등 기본어휘	중등 기본어휘	확장 어휘	표제어 수
Unit 1 The Fortune	Lesson 1 A Rich Boy	year, week, young, nothing, homeless	hire, court, dozen, charity, fortune, without, customer	mow, blanket	28
	Lesson 2 A Smart Invention	weak, maybe, doorbell	earn, trap, connect, delivery, hesitate, cell phone, invention	burglar, millionaire, make angry, run errands	
Unit 2 The Bat	Lesson 1 The Lives of Bats	bat, sound	hang, death, raise, symbol, however, western, familiar	flap, prey, grasp, bounce, mammal	28
	Lesson 2 The Wonderful Flier of the Night	flier, mouse, pocket	calm, cave, harm, island, shadow, ceiling, village	dangle, lonely, memorial, upside down	
Unit 3 Around the World	Lesson 1 New Year's Day	past, sweet, country, receive, calendar	fancy, delight, envelope, exchange, festival, tradition	bamboo, countdown, firecracker	28
	Lesson 2 Losing a Tooth Customs	gold, excuse, present, put in	wrap, loose	crow, couch, pillow, wiggle, show up, be about to, come out of, fall asleep	
Unit 4 Life Cycle	Lesson 1 The Life Cycle of a Frog	frog, again, life cycle, look like, be covered with	lay, lung, complete	gills, hatch, froglet, tadpole, amphibian, germinate	28
	Lesson 2 Turn Back Time	age, new, why, ugly	avoid, accept, behave, explain, whenever, apologize, recognize, turn back, look down on	unbelievable	
Unit 5 Space	Lesson 1 From the Earth to the Moon	fine, moon, near, circle	data, deal, event, launch, finally, history, astronaut	alarm, footprint, spacecraft	28
	Lesson 2 Fly Me to Mars	hill, plate, holiday	beg, space, discuss, suggest, equipment, spacesuit	Mars, alien, weird, satellite, telescope	

사용 연령 : 초등학생 이상

5권		초등 기본어휘	중등 기본어휘	확장 어휘	표제어 수
Unit 6 The Ocean	Lesson 1 The Life of a Salmon	rock, salt	fail, male, adult, enter, female, return, stream, several, survive	salmon, instinct, migration	28
	Lesson 2 Pirates and Treasure	away, ship, often	area, sweep, search, captain, terrible, threaten, treasure, passenger	cruise, pirate, take over	
Unit 7 Great Adventures	Lesson 1 The Second to Reach the South Pole	a few, run out of	shore, suffer, attempt, prepare, succeed, vehicle, national, the English	polar, exhausted, frostbite, expedition	28
	Lesson 2 The Mystery of the Devil's Triangle	theater, daughter, triangle, draw into	press, reason, screen, situation, get worse	hero, bubble, bacteria, submarine, whirlpool	
Unit 8 The Honor	Lesson 1 The Nobel Prize	corner	cash, honor, since, wealth, consist, physics, ceremony, establish, literature, anniversary, international	more than, be noted for	28
	Lesson 2 The Funny Winner	know, correct, question	chance, advance, mistake, confident, everybody, dictionary, competition, participate, break wind	bloat, giggle	
Unit 9 Step Back in Time	Lesson 1 The Lost City of Pompeii	bath, shop, mountain	bury, remain, disaster, preserve, ash	erupt, later, petrify, uncover, volcano, archaeologist	28
	Lesson 2 The Stone Age	clock, knife, point	raw, set, edge, spin, tool, faint, sharp, create, wonder, surround	Stone Age	
Unit 10 World Landmark	Lesson 1 The Leaning Tower of Pisa	finish	bell, lean, cease, belong, degree, effort, vertical, foundation, remarkable, construction, even though	marble, unstable	28
	Lesson 2 Climbing a Bridge	early, bridge	rope, shock, steep, tight, beside, neighbor, on air, walk across	landmark, guardrail, mind one's step, miss one's step	

Contents

Wow! Smart Vocabulary

5

Unit 1
The Fortune

✪ 초등 기본어휘 ◯ 중등 기본어휘 △ 확장어휘

1
✪ **year**
명 해, 1년, 나이

2
✪ **week**
명 주, 일주일

3
✪ **young**
형 어린, 젊은
반 old 늙은

4
✪ **nothing**
대 아무것도 아닌 것
반 everything 모든 것

5
✪ **homeless**
형 집 없는
❶ the homeless
집 없는 사람들

6
◯ **hire**
동 고용하다
반 fire 해고하다

7
◯ **court**
명 코트, 경기장

8
◯ **dozen**
명 12개짜리 한 묶음, 다스

9
◯ **charity**
명 자선, 자선 단체

10
◯ **fortune**
명 재산, 부, 행운
유 wealth 부

11
◯ **without**
전 ~없이
반 with ~와 함께

12
◯ **customer**
명 손님, 고객

13
△ **mow**
동 (풀을) 베다
유 clip (가위 등으로) 자르다, 깎다
구 mow the lawn 잔디를 깎다

14
△ **blanket**
명 담요

 주어진 뜻을 잘 읽고, 빈칸에 해당하는 단어를 쓰세요.

1. a person who buys something at a shop → c_____
2. 365 days or 12 months → y_____
3. having no home → h_____
4. to cut grass → m_____
5. a place where games such as tennis are played → c_____
6. from Monday to Sunday → w_____
7. an organization to raise money to help people → c_____
8. not old → y_____
9. twelve or something in a group of twelve → d_____
10. a large piece of cloth to keep you warm → b_____

B 연관되는 단어를 알아보고, 빈칸에 영어 또는 우리말 뜻을 쓰세요.

| _____ a clerk | _____ 동 고용하다 | ↔ | fire 동 _____ |

점원을 고용하다

| _____ a reason | _____ 전 ~ 없어 | ↔ | 전 ~와 함께 _____ |

이유 없이

| make a _____ | _____ 명 재산, 부 | = | wealth 명 _____ |

부자가 되다

| come to _____ | 대 아무것도 아닌 것 _____ | ↔ | 대 _____ |

(노력이) 수포로 돌아가다

빈칸에 알맞은 단어를 쓰고, 사다리를 타고 내려가 정답을 확인하세요.

1. I bought a _____ apples.

2. Let's go to the tennis _____.

3. The company will _____ new workers.

4. He works 40 hours a _____.

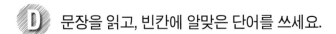

hire   week   dozen   court

D

문장을 읽고, 빈칸에 알맞은 단어를 쓰세요.

1. Julia is _____ the lawn.   줄리아는 잔디를 깎고 있다.

2. I met her ten _____ ago.   나는 10년 전에 그녀를 만났다.

3. She was a _____ girl at that time.   그 당시에 그녀는 어린 소녀였다.

4. Although time has gone by, _____ has changed.
   시간이 흘렀어도 아무것도 변한 게 없다.

5. She has her own store and makes a _____.
   그녀는 자신의 가게를 가지고 있고 큰 돈을 번다.

6. Lots of _____ come into her store.   많은 손님들이 그녀의 가게에 온다.

7. She is doing it _____ any help.   그녀는 어떠한 도움도 없이 그 일을 하고 있다.

8. One day, she saw some _____ people.   어느 날 그녀는 노숙자들을 보았다.

9. She gave them some _____.   그녀는 그들에게 담요를 주었다.

10. She has given money to _____ for the homeless since then.
    그녀는 그때부터 노숙자들을 위해 자선 단체들에 돈을 기부하고 있다.

 빈칸에 알맞은 단어를 단어 박스에서 찾아 넣어 이야기를 완성하세요.

A Rich Boy

Ryan Ross is a 9-_____-old boy who runs his own business.

When he was three years old, he sold 20 _____ fresh eggs.

He made about 50 dollars a we_____.

Later, he had a lawn-_____ business.

He was too yo_____ to mow lawns.

So he h_____ older kids to mow for 15 dollars an hour.

He charged his cu_____ 20 dollars an hour.

He made 5 dollars an hour _____ doing any work.

After that, he made a _____ in his power-washing business*.

Now, he has six buildings.

He has a hockey rink and a basketball _____.

He also runs a c_____.

He collects _____ to help the _____.

His big dream is to buy his own hockey team.

He says, "_____ is stopping me.

What's stopping you?"

*power-washing business 강력 세척사업

Word Box

dozen · hired · year · customers · mowing · young · blankets · without · fortune · court · charity · homeless · Nothing · week

• Lesson 2 • A Smart Invention

1
⭐ **weak**
형 약한, 허약한
반 strong 강한

2
⭐ **maybe**
부 아마, 어쩌면

3
⭐ **doorbell**
명 초인종

4
○ **earn**
동 (돈을) 벌다, 얻다

5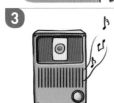
○ **trap**
명 덫, 함정, 계략
동 덫으로 잡다, 가두다

6
○ **connect**
동 연결하다
명 connection 연결

7
○ **delivery**
명 배달
동 deliver 배달하다

8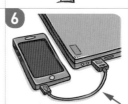
○ **hesitate**
동 망설이다, 주저하다
명 hesitation 주저, 망설임

9
○ **cell phone**
명 휴대 전화
유 mobile phone 휴대 전화

10
○ **invention**
명 발명(품)
동 invent 발명하다

11
△ **burglar**
명 강도, 절도범
유 thief 도둑

12
△ **millionaire**
명 백만장자

13
△ **make angry**
구 화나게 하다, 약 올리다
유 get a rise out of
~을 약 올리다

14
△ **run errands**
구 심부름하다
유 do an errand,
go on an errand
심부름가다

A 주어진 뜻을 잘 읽고, 빈칸에 해당하는 단어나 구를 쓰세요.

1. something to use to catch a mouse → t_____
2. not certain → m_____
3. to join together → c_____
4. a person who enters a house to steal something → b_____
5. the action of taking goods or letters to people → d_____
6. a button outside a house → d_____
7. to be slow to speak or act in doubt → h_____
8. to offend a person → m_____
9. not physically strong → w_____
10. to make a short trip to do things for a person → r_____

B 다음 장면에 어울리는 단어를 넣어 문장을 완성하세요.

| cell phone | inventions | earned | millionaire |

1. He was interested in _____.
2. He finally invented the _____.
3. He _____ a lot of money.
4. He became a _____.

C 문장을 읽고, 빈칸에 알맞은 뜻을 쓴 후 해당하는 것을 선으로 연결하세요.

trap Go!

명 함정, 계략 •

동 가두다 •

명 덫 •

• It's a mouse trap.
  이것은 쥐_____이다.

• He fell into a trap.
  그는 _____에 빠졌다.

• She was trapped in the car.
  그녀는 차 안에 _____.

D 문장을 읽고, 빈칸에 알맞은 단어를 쓰세요.

1. I want to be a _____. 나는 백만장자가 되고 싶다.

2. I worked for a flower _____ shop. 나는 꽃 배달 가게에서 일했다.

3. But the owner _____ me _____, so I quit the job.
   하지만 가게 주인이 나를 화나게 해서 나는 일을 그만 두었다.

4. Now, I _____ _____ for pocket money. 요즘, 나는 용돈을 받고 심부름을 간다.

5. But it isn't enough to _____ a lot of money.
   하지만 이것은 많은 돈을 벌기에는 충분하지 않다.

6. I decided to catch a _____ to get the reward money.
   나는 포상금을 받기 위해 강도를 잡기로 결심했다.

7. I set a _____, which was _____ to a deep hole.
   내가 만든 함정은 깊은 구멍과 연결되어 있었다.

8. I think it's a great _____. 나는 이것이 위대한 발명품이라고 생각한다.

9. But, when I caught the thief, I was too _____.
   그러나, 내가 도둑을 잡았을 때, 나는 너무 약했다.

10. I wanted to call the police, but I didn't have a _____ _____.
    경찰에게 전화를 하고 싶었지만 나는 휴대 전화를 가지고 있지 않았다.

11. I rang the _____ to ask for help, but nobody was at home.
    나는 도움을 청하기 위해 초인종을 눌렀지만 아무도 집에 있지 않았다.

12. He got away because I _____. 그는 내가 망설여서 도망가버렸다.

13. _____ I'll be able to catch a thief next time.
    아마도 나는 다음에 도둑을 잡을 수 있을 것이다.

E 빈칸에 알맞은 단어를 단어 박스에서 찾아 넣어 이야기를 완성하세요.

A Smart Invention

Ted's mom complains,

"I've got some missing de_____.

_____ somebody took them."

Every day, Ted hides and waits for the _____

One day, a tall man comes to his house.

He rings the _____ to see if anyone is at home.

Then, he whistles and takes Ted's delivery.

Ted wants to _____ him _____.

He c_____ the doorbell to his c_____ _____.

The burglar comes back when Ted goes out to _____ some _____

He rings the doorbell again, and Ted answers his cell phone.

Ted says, "I'm so old and _____.

Can you come in and help me?"

The burglar _____ a little but tries to steal things in the house.

"Oh, no!" The burglar is _____ in a net,

and the police officers come.

The next morning, Ted's mom says,

"Ted, you're in the newspaper."

People buy his smart _____.

He _____ a lot of money and becomes a m_____ e.

Word Box

Maybe	cell phone	deliveries	doorbell	burglar
weak	connects	millionaire	trapped	run ~ errands
invention	earns	hesitates	make ~ angry

Unit 2
The Bat

• Lesson 1 • *The Lives of Bats*

 초등 기본어휘   중등 기본어휘 확장어휘

1 ⭐ **bat**
⊛ 박쥐
❍ vampire bat 흡혈 박쥐

2 ⭐ **sound**
⊛ 소리, 음
⊛ 소리를 내다, ~하게 들리다
⊕ noise 소음
❍ sound wave 음파

3  ◇ **hang**
⊛ 걸다, 매달리다
⊕ suspend 매달다, 걸다
dangle 매달리다, 매달다
(과거형 / 과거분사형: hung)

4 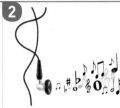 ◇ **death**
⊛ 죽음
⊛ dead 죽은
❍ sudden death 갑작스런 죽음

5  ◇ **raise**
⊛ 기르다
⊕ bring up, rear
기르다, 양육하다

6 ◇ **symbol**
⊛ 상징
⊕ image 상, sign 기호

7  ◇ **however**
⊛ 그러나
⊕ but, though 그러나, 하지만

8  ◇ **western**
⊛ 서쪽의
⊛ west 서쪽
⊛ Western 서양의
❍ Western Europe 서유럽

9  ◇ **familiar**
⊛ 친한, 잘 아는, 익숙한
⊛ unfamiliar 잘 모르는, 익숙하지 않은

10  ◇ **flap**
⊛ 펄럭이다, (날개를) 퍼덕이다
⊕ flutter 펄럭이다
⊙ flap away 날개를 치며 날아가 버리다

11  ◇ **prey**
⊛ 먹이
⊛ 잡아먹다
⊙ prey on ~을 잡아먹다

12  ◇ **grasp**
⊛ 꽉 잡다, 움켜잡다
⊕ grab, hold, catch 잡다

13  ◇ **bounce**
⊛ 튀다, (소리가) 반사하다
⊙ bounce up 펄쩍 뛰다
⊙ bounce back (병으로부터) 회복하다

14  ◇ **mammal**
⊛ 포유동물
❍ marine mammal 해양 포유동물

A 주어진 뜻을 잘 읽고, 빈칸에 해당하는 단어를 쓰세요.

1. to care for a child or young animal → r_____
2. the end of life → d_____
3. the west part of the world → w_____
4. a thing that represents something → s_____
5. to move upwards from a surface after hitting a ball → b_____
6. to move quickly up and down → f_____
7. something that you hear → s_____
8. an animal that is hunted → p_____
9. an animal like a mouse with wings → b_____
10. an animal that gives birth to babies like humans → m_____

B 연관되는 단어를 알아보고, 빈칸에 영어 또는 우리말 뜻을 쓰세요.

_____ your hat on the hook.
모자를 옷걸이에 걸어라.
_____ 통 매달다 = suspend 통 _____

a _____ friend
친한 친구
_____ 형 친한 ↔ _____ 형 잘 모르는

_____ his hand
그의 손을 꽉 잡다
_____ 통 꽉 잡다 = hold 통 _____

_____, I can't understand it.
그러나 나는 그것을 이해할 수 없다.
_____ 부 그러나 = _____ 접 그러나, 하지만

빈칸에 알맞은 단어를 쓰고, 사다리를 타고 내려가 정답을 확인하세요.

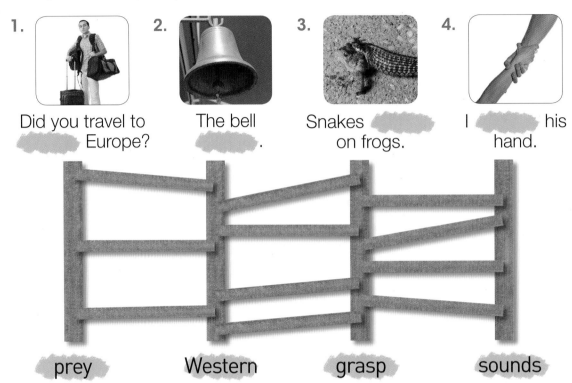

1. Did you travel to _____ Europe?

2. The bell _____ .

3. Snakes _____ on frogs.

4. I _____ his hand.

prey　　　Western　　　grasp　　　sounds

D 문장을 읽고, 빈칸에 알맞은 단어를 쓰세요.

1. It is a kind of _____. 이것은 포유동물의 한 종류이다.

2. It has wings and can _____ them. 이것은 날개를 가지고 있어서 날갯짓을 할 수 있다.

3. It usually _____ upside down. 이것은 보통 거꾸로 매달려 있다.

4. Can you guess what it is? It's a _____. 무엇인지 추측할 수 있는가? 이것은 박쥐다.

5. I _____ it when I was young. 나는 어렸을 때 이것을 길렀다.

6. So I'm very _____ with bats. 그래서 나는 박쥐에 매우 익숙하다.

7. My friend John _____ a ball. He saw a bat.
내 친구 존은 공을 튕기고 있었다. 그는 박쥐를 보았다.

8. He said it's a _____ of bad luck. 그는 그것이 불운을 상징한다고 말했다.

9. It is connected with _____. 그것은 죽음과 관련되어 있다.

10. _____, I didn't believe him. 그러나 나는 그의 말을 믿지 않았다.

 빈칸에 알맞은 단어를 단어 박스에서 찾아 넣어 이야기를 완성하세요.

The Lives of Bats

_____ are found almost everywhere in the world.

But people aren't _____ with them. What about you? Do you like bats?

They are the only _____ that can fly.

They can _____ by spreading out their wings.

Many bats live in trees by h_____ on the branches.

Some of them live in caves.

They are perfect places to _____ babies and to sleep during the day.

They use their ears when they catch their _____ at night.

When bats fly, they make some so_____.

Those sounds hit insects, and the echoes _____ back to the bats.

The bats fly fast and _____ the insects.

They help farmers by eating insects and saving crops.

Bats are a _____ of _____ in _____ culture.

_____, bats are a symbol of happiness in China.

Word Box

grasp	Bats	Western	familiar	However
sounds	death	mammals	symbol	bounce
hanging	flap	prey	raise	

• Lesson 2 • *The Wonderful Flier of the Night*

✪ 초등 기본어휘 ◯ 중등 기본어휘 ⬡ 확장어휘

1  ✪ **flier**
명 하늘을 나는 것, 비행사
동 fly 날다
➡ jet flier 제트기 비행사

2  ✪ **mouse**
명 쥐
복 mice 쥐들
➡ field mouse 들쥐

3  ✪ **pocket**
명 (호)주머니, 써야 할 돈
형 포켓용의, 소형의
➡ pocket money 용돈

4  ◯ **calm**
형 고요한, 차분한
반 excited 흥분한
➡ calm down 진정하다

5  ◯ **cave**
명 동굴
➡ hollow a cave 굴을 파다

6  ◯ **harm**
동 해치다, 손상시키다
유 hurt, injure 상처 입히다

7  ◯ **island**
명 섬
➡ coral island 산호섬
➡ desert island 무인도

8  ◯ **shadow**
명 그림자
형 shadowy 그늘이 진, 어둑어둑한

9 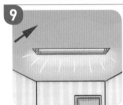 ◯ **ceiling**
명 천장
➡ ceiling lamp 천장 등

10  ◯ **village**
명 마을
➡ global village 지구촌

11  ⬡ **dangle**
동 매달리다
유 hang 매달리다
➡ dangle from the ceiling 천장에 매달려 있다

12  ⬡ **lonely**
형 외로운, 쓸쓸한
➡ feel lonely 외롭다

13  ⬡ **memorial**
명 기념물, 기념비
명 memory 기억, 기념, 추억
동 memorize 기억하다

14  ⬡ **upside down**
부 거꾸로
➡ turn the table upside down 탁자를 뒤집어 엎다

 A 주어진 뜻을 잘 읽고, 빈칸에 해당하는 단어를 쓰세요.

1. to hang or swing → d_____

2. a dark shape made when something is between the light and a surface → s_____

3. the top of a room → c_____

4. a large hole in a hill or under the ground → c_____

5. something that can fly → f_____

6. a small piece of land surrounded by water → i_____

7. to hurt or injure → h_____

8. not excited or nervous → c_____

9. when the bottom and the top are reversed → u_____

10. something built to honor the memory of a person or an event → m_____

 B 다음 장면에 어울리는 단어를 넣어 문장을 완성하세요.

| pocket | mice | village | lonely |

1. A boy lives in a small _____.

2. He doesn't have any friends. He bought some _____.

3. He always carries them in his _____.

4. He is not _____ anymore.

C 문장을 읽고, 빈칸에 알맞은 뜻을 쓴 후 해당하는 것을 선으로 연결하세요.

pocket

(명) 주머니 •

(형) 포켓용의 •

(명) 돈, 금전 •

Go!

• He has an empty pocket.
그는 _____ 이 하나도 없다.

• She has a pocket dictionary.
그녀는 _____ 사전을 가지고 있다.

• I put the key in my coat pocket.
나는 코트 _____ 에 열쇠를 넣었다.

D 문장을 읽고, 빈칸에 알맞은 단어를 쓰세요.

1. There is an _____ . 섬 하나가 있다.

2. On the island is a small _____ . 그 섬에 작은 마을이 하나 있다.

3. You can see an interesting _____ there. 너는 거기서 흥미로운 기념비를 볼 수 있다.

4. A long time ago, a _____ boy lived there.
오래 전에 외로운 소년 한 명이 그곳에 살았다.

5. One day, he saw a _____ . 어느 날, 그는 그림자 하나를 보았다.

6. He followed it and came to a _____ . 그는 그것을 따라 동굴로 갔다.

7. He saw something on the _____ . 그는 천장에 있는 무언가를 보았다.

8. It _____ from a lamp. 그것은 램프에 매달려 있었다.

9. It was _____ _____ . 그것은 거꾸로 뒤집혀 있었다.

10. The boy got closer, but it stayed _____ .
소년은 더 가까이 갔지만, 그것은 가만히 있었다.

11. He said, "I won't _____ you." "널 해치지 않을게."라고 그는 말했다.

12. He put it in his _____ and went back home.
그는 그것을 자기 주머니에 넣고 집으로 돌아왔다.

13. When he showed it to people, some said it was a _____ .
그가 그것을 사람들에게 보여줬을 때, 몇몇은 그것이 날아다니는 거라고 말했다.

14. Others said it looked like a _____ . 다른 사람들은 그것이 쥐같이 생겼다고 말했다.

 빈칸에 알맞은 단어를 단어 박스에서 찾아 넣어 이야기를 완성하세요.

The Wonderful Flier of the Night

Ted takes a trip to an _____ .

People say, "Don't go to the _____ .

A vampire bat will get you and _____ you."

But he goes into the cave to study some insects.

He looks up at the ce_____ .

Something is _____ .

It is _____ _____ in the cave.

Both of them are very scared but stay c_____ .

It spreads its wings and makes a big s_____ .

Ted says, "Oh, you're a _____ bat. I will be your friend."

He opens his _____ , and the vampire bat goes inside.

They go down to the _____ .

Big _____ are bothering and biting people in the town.

The vampire bat flies up and traps them with its wings.

One day, the vampire bat disappeared.

To remember it, they built a me_____ for the vampire bat:

The Wonderful _____ of the Night.

Word Box

memorial   ceiling   mice   island   lonely

shadow   cave   pocket   harm   village

dangling   upside down   Flier   calm

Unit 3
Around the World

• Lesson 1 • *New Year's Day*

⭐ 초등 기본어휘 ◯ 중등 기본어휘 🔺 확장어휘

1
⭐ **past**
형 과거의, 지나간
명 과거
반 future 미래
구 in the past 과거에

2
⭐ **sweet**
형 달콤한
명 단 것, 사탕 및 초콜릿류
반 bitter (맛이) 쓴
◯ sweet candy 달콤한 사탕

3
⭐ **country**
명 나라, 시골
유 nation, kingdom 나라, 국가

4
⭐ **receive**
동 받다
명 receipt 영수증
유 get, accept 받다

5
⭐ **calendar**
명 달력
◯ solar calendar 양력
◯ lunar calendar 음력

6
◯ **fancy**
형 화려한, 공상의
반 plain 평범한, 단조로운

7
◯ **delight**
동 매우 기쁘게 하다
명 기쁨
형 delighted 아주 기뻐하는
유 please 기쁘게 하다

8
◯ **envelope**
명 봉투
동 envelop 감싸다

9
◯ **exchange**
동 교환하다
명 교환
◯ exchange student
교환 학생

10
◯ **festival**
명 축제
구 hold a festival 축제를 열다

11
◯ **tradition**
명 전통
형 traditional 전통의
유 custom 관습

12
🔺 **bamboo**
명 대나무
◯ bamboo basket
대나무로 만든 바구니

13
🔺 **countdown**
명 초읽기, 카운트다운
구 begin a countdown
초읽기를 시작하다

14
🔺 **firecracker**
명 폭죽
유 firework 폭죽

 주어진 뜻을 잘 읽고, 빈칸에 해당하는 단어를 쓰세요.

1. before the present → p_____
2. something that shows days, weeks, and months → c_____
3. to make someone happy → d_____
4. very colorful and decorative → f_____
5. to give and receive something → e_____
6. a tall plant that is empty inside → b_____
7. counting backward from ten to one → c_____
8. a paper cover which you put a letter → e_____
9. celebrating a special day or event → f_____
10. the taste of sugar → s_____

B 연관되는 단어를 알아보고, 빈칸에 영어 또는 우리말 뜻을 쓰세요.

all over the _____
전국에서
_____ 명 나라 = _____ 명 나라, 국가

_____ a letter
편지를 받다
_____ 동 받다 = accept 동 _____

follow _____
전통을 따르다
_____ 명 전통 = _____ 명 관습

A _____ goes off.
폭죽이 터진다.
_____ 명 폭죽 = _____ 명 폭죽

C 빈칸에 알맞은 단어를 쓰고, 사다리를 타고 내려가 정답을 확인하세요.

1. This basket is made of _____.

2. Your dress is _____.

3. Don't eat too many _____.

4. Do you have an _____?

sweets   bamboo   envelope   fancy

D 문장을 읽고, 빈칸에 알맞은 단어를 쓰세요.

1. I found an old _____ in a drawer. 나는 서랍 안에서 오래된 달력을 발견했다.

2. I looked back on the _____. 나는 과거를 회상했다.

3. In May, I _____ a birthday present from my parents.
5월에 나는 부모님으로부터 생일 선물을 받았다.

4. It _____ me. 그것은 나를 기쁘게 했다.

5. At Christmas, my family _____ gifts according to _____.
크리스마스에 우리 가족은 전통에 따라 선물을 교환했다.

6. My family went to a _____ on December 31.
12월 31일에 우리 가족은 축제에 갔다.

7. There were a lot of people from all over the _____.
전국에서 모인 많은 사람들이 있었다.

8. We enjoyed lighting _____. 우리는 폭죽 놀이를 즐겼다.

9. The last day of the year ended with the _____.
그 해의 마지막 날은 카운트다운과 함께 마무리되었다.

 빈칸에 알맞은 단어를 단어 박스에서 찾아 넣어 이야기를 완성하세요.

New Year's Day

People happily wish others good luck on New Year's Day. They look back on the _____ year and plan for the coming new year. People all over the world celebrate the new year in different ways. They celebrate the new year with _____ from their c_____.

Japanese people send and _____ New Year's cards and share warm wishes. They decorate their homes with _____ and pine branches.

In Mexico, people eat 12 grapes when the midnight c_____ begins. Each of the _____ grapes stands for good luck for each month of the new year.

A fe_____ is an important part of the New Year's celebration in Brazil. People sing and dance while dressed in _____ clothes.

Chinese people celebrate New Year's Day on the lunar*_____.

They put lucky money in red en_____. Then, they _____ them as gifts for the new year. They also light f_____ and enjoy lion dances in the street.

What New Year's Day celebration in your country _____ you?

*lunar 음력의

Word Box

calendar   firecrackers   festival   traditions   sweet

bamboo   envelopes   fancy   exchange   receive

countdown   countries   past   delights

✪ 초등 기본어휘 ◐ 중등 기본어휘 △ 확장어휘

1 ✪ **gold**

- 형 금의, 금으로 만든
- 명 금
- 형 golden 금빛의, 금의

2 ✪ **excuse**

- 동 용서하다, 봐주다
- 명 변명

3 ✪ **present**

- 명 선물, 현재, 지금
- 형 출석한, 참석한, 현재의

4 ✪ **put in**

- 구 ~에 넣다
- 반 take out 꺼내다

5 ◐ **wrap**

- 동 감싸다, 포장하다
- 명 덮개, 포장지
- ◐ wrapping paper 포장지

6 ◐ **loose**

- 형 헐거운, 느슨한
- ◐ loose tooth 흔들리는 치아

7 △ **crow**

- 명 까마귀

8 △ **couch**

- 명 소파, 긴 의자
- ◐ couch potato 소파에 앉아 TV만 보는 게으른 사람

9 △ **pillow**

- 명 베개
- ◐ pillow fight 베개 싸움

10 △ **wiggle**

- 동 흔들다, 움직이다
- 명 몸부림

11 △ **show up**

- 구 나타나다
- 유 appear, turn up 나타나다

12 △ **be about to**

- 구 막 ~하려는 참이다
- 구 be just about to do something 이제 막 ~하려는 참이다

13 △ **come out of**

- 구 ~에서 나오다

14 △ **fall asleep**

- 구 잠들다
- 유 drop asleep 잠들다

A 주어진 뜻을 잘 읽고, 빈칸에 해당하는 단어나 구를 쓰세요.

1. to appear at a place → s__________
2. a sofa → c__________
3. a black bird → c__________
4. to move up and down or from side to side → w__________
5. to cover something → w__________
6. a gift → p__________
7. not tight → l__________
8. to be going to do something soon → b__________
9. a cushion that you put your head on → p__________
10. to go to dreamland → f__________

B 다음 장면에 어울리는 단어나 구를 넣어 문장을 완성하세요.

gold	Excuse	came out of	put in

1. On my way home, a man came up to me. "__________ me. Is this yours?"
2. "It __________ __________ __________ your pocket."
3. It was my __________ watch.
4. I said, "Thank you very much," and __________ it __________ my bag.

C 문장을 읽고, 빈칸에 알맞은 뜻을 쓴 후 해당하는 것을 선으로 연결하세요.

present

(형) 출석한, 참석한 •

(명) 선물 •

Go!

(명) 현재, 지금 •

• I am satisfied with my life at present.
나는 _____ 내 생활에 만족한다.

• He was present at the meeting.
그는 회의에 _____.

• She got a birthday present.
그녀는 생일 _____을 받았다.

D 문장을 읽고, 빈칸에 알맞은 단어를 쓰세요.

1. Jack bought a _____ for Rose. 잭은 로즈를 위한 선물을 샀다.

2. It was a _____ ring. 그것은 금반지였다.

3. He _____ it _____ a box, and _____ it.
그는 그것을 상자 안에 넣어 포장했다.

4. He waited until she _____ _____. 그는 그녀가 나타날 때까지 기다렸다.

5. She _____ _____ _____ school. 그녀가 학교에서 나왔다.

6. He said, "_____ me. Where are you going?"
"잠깐만. 어디 가는 중이니?"라고 그가 말했다.

7. She said, "I _____ _____ _____ go home."
"막 집에 가려는 참이야."라고 그녀가 말했다.

8. They sat on a _____, and he gave her the gift.
그들은 소파에 앉았고, 그는 그녀에게 선물을 주었다.

9. That night, he put his head on the _____. 그날 밤, 그는 베개에 머리를 뉘였다.

10. There was a picture of a _____ on it. 그것 위에는 까마귀 그림이 있었다.

11. He couldn't _____ _____. 그는 잠들 수가 없었다.

12. He worried, "What if the ring is too _____?"
'만약 반지가 너무 헐거우면 어떡하지?'라고 그는 걱정했다.

13. Suddenly, he felt something _____. 갑자기, 그는 무엇인가가 움직이는 것을 느꼈다.

E 빈칸에 알맞은 단어를 단어 박스에서 찾아 넣어 이야기를 완성하세요.

Losing a Tooth Customs

Tom invites some friends from different countries to his house.

At lunch, Ted says to his friends, "My tooth is _____. It _____ _____ _____ fall out."

He wi_____ his tooth with his finger. Then, it _____ _____ _____ his mouth.

Marco from Spain says, "Oh, _____ your tooth _____ a mouse hole.

The Tooth Mouse will take it and give you a p_____."

Nana from Greece says, "No, no. Throw it on the roof.

A cr_____ will take it and give you a strong, new one."

Right after dinner, Ted puts his tooth under his pi_____.

He lies on the _____. He _____ _____ quickly.

Tara, the Tooth Fairy,* _____ _____ and tries to take his tooth.

Tara says, "_____ me. Can I take your tooth?"

Ted wakes up and says sleepily, "No problem. I'll give it to you."

The Tooth Fairy _____ the tooth in paper.

The Tooth Fairy gives _____ coins to Ted.

*__Tooth Fairy__ 이의 요정

Word Box

gold	wiggles	Excuse	present	couch
wraps	comes out of	shows up	loose	put ~ in
crow	falls asleep	is about to		pillow

Unit 4
Life Cycle

• Lesson 1 • *The Life Cycle of a Frog*

⭐ 초등 기본어휘 ◯ 중등 기본어휘 ⬣ 확장어휘

1
⭐ **frog**
명 개구리
➡ green frog 청개구리
cf. toad 두꺼비

2
⭐ **again**
부 다시, 한 번 더
구 again and again 되풀이하여

3
⭐ **life cycle**
명 생활 주기
cf. cycle 순환, 주기
➡ family life cycle
   가족 생활 주기

4
⭐ **look like**
구 ~처럼 보이다, ~와 비슷하다
유 seem ~처럼 보이다

5
⭐ **be covered with**
구 ~으로 뒤덮이다
동 cover 덮다
구 be covered with snow
   눈으로 뒤덮이다

6
◯ **lay**
동 (알을) 낳다, 놓다, 눕히다
유 spawn 알을 낳다

7
◯ **lung**
명 폐, 허파
➡ lung cancer 폐암

8
◯ **complete**
형 완전한, 완성한
동 끝마치다
반 incomplete 불완전한
부 completely 완전히

9
⬣ **gills**
명 (보통 복수형) 아가미

10
⬣ **hatch**
동 부화하다, (알을) 깨다

11
⬣ **froglet**
명 새끼 개구리

12
⬣ **tadpole**
명 올챙이

13
⬣ **amphibian**
명 양서류
형 양서류의

14
⬣ **germinate**
동 싹트다, 싹트게 하다

A 주어진 뜻을 잘 읽고, 빈칸에 해당하는 단어나 구를 쓰세요.

1. a young frog without legs   → t_____
2. to come out of an egg   → h_____
3. a baby frog   → f_____
4. the body part that you use for breathing   → l_____
5. the changes that is from birth to death   → l_____
6. to be spread or topped with something   → b_____
7. one more time   → a_____
8. a cold-blooded animal living on land and in water   → a_____
9. the body parts for fish to use to breathe   → g_____
10. to sprout or begin to grow   → g_____

B 연관되는 단어를 알아보고, 빈칸에 영어 또는 우리말 뜻을 쓰세요.

_____ an egg ～ _____ ⑧ 낳다 = **spawn** ⑧ _____
알을 낳다

He _____ _____ a movie star. ～ _____ ㉠ ～처럼 보이다 = _____ ⑧ ～처럼 보이다
그는 영화배우처럼 보인다.

A _____ jumped high. ～ _____ ⑲ 개구리 → _____ ⑲ 두꺼비
개구리는 높이 뛰었다.

The plan is _____. ～ _____ ⑱ 완전한, 완성한 ↔ _____ ⑱ 불완전한
그 계획이 완성되었다.

C 빈칸에 알맞은 단어를 쓰고, 사다리를 타고 내려가 정답을 확인하세요.

1.
New leaves _____.

2.
The town _____ snow.

3.
A _____ is swimming in the pond.

4.
An egg is about to _____.

is covered with   hatch   germinate   tadpole

D 문장을 읽고, 빈칸에 알맞은 단어를 쓰세요.

1. My science homework is _____.   내 과학 숙제가 완성되었다.

2. I learned about _____ today.   나는 오늘 양서류들에 대해서 배웠다.

3. A _____ is an amphibian.   개구리는 양서류이다.

4. It _____ _____ a toad.   그것은 두꺼비와 비슷하게 생겼다.

5. I studied its _____ _____ for homework.
   나는 숙제로 그것의 생활 주기를 조사했다.

6. After finishing it, I read it _____.   숙제를 끝내고 나는 그것을 다시 읽어 보았다.

7. Frogs _____ eggs. Tadpoles come out of the eggs.
   개구리는 알을 낳는다. 올챙이들이 알에서 나온다.

8. Tadpoles breathe with their _____.   올챙이는 아가미로 숨을 쉰다.

9. They become _____.   그들은 새끼 개구리가 된다.

10. Frogs breathe with their _____.   개구리는 폐로 숨을 쉰다.

 빈칸에 알맞은 단어를 단어 박스에서 찾아 넣어 이야기를 완성하세요.

The Life Cycle of a Frog

In Spring, seeds _____ and flowers bloom.

"Ribbit! Ribbit!" A _____ is in the pond.

A frog is an _____. A frog _____ many eggs in the water.

Frog eggs _____ _____ _____ a jellylike coating.

About 6 to 21 days later, the eggs _____.

7 to 10 days later, a _____ begins to swim.

After about 6 to 9 weeks, little legs start to sprout.

A tadpole breathes with its gi_____ in the water.

As it grows, the gills disappear, and lu_____ form.

After about 9 weeks, a tadpole _____ _____ a young frog with a tail. We call it a _____.

By 12 to 16 weeks, a frog's growth is _____.

The frog lays eggs in the water, and the cycle begins _____.

The _____ _____ of a frog continues.

Word Box

life cycle | looks like | tadpole | frog | complete

froglet | are covered with | again | germinate | gills | amphibian

lays | hatch | lungs

• Lesson 2 • Turn Back Time

★ 초등 기본어휘 ◇ 중등 기본어휘 △ 확장어휘

1

★ **age**
명 나이, 시기, 시대
구 act one's age
나이에 걸맞게 행동하다

2

★ **new**
형 새로운
명 새로운 것
반 old 오래된

3

★ **why**
부 왜, 어째서, ~한 이유
구 tell me why
이유를 나에게 말하다

4

★ **ugly**
형 못생긴, 추한
반 beautiful 아름다운
○ ugly face 못생긴 얼굴

5

◇ **avoid**
동 피하다
유 keep away from
~을 멀리하다

6

◇ **accept**
동 받아들이다, 인정하다,
수락하다
형 acceptable 받아들일 수 있는
반 refuse 거절하다

7

◇ **behave**
동 행동하다, 처신하다
명 behavior 행동
구 behave well 잘 처신하다

8

◇ **explain**
동 설명하다
명 explanation 설명
유 describe 묘사하다, 설명하다

9

◇ **whenever**
접 ~할 때마다

10

◇ **apologize**
동 사과하다
명 apology 사과
구 apologize for
~에 대해 사과하다

11

◇ **recognize**
동 알아보다, 인식하다
명 recognition 알아봄, 인식

12

◇ **turn back**
구 되돌아오다, 되돌리다
구 turn back from
~에서 돌아오다

13

◇ **look down on**
구 ~을 낮추어 보다, 업신여기다
구 look down upon a
person 사람을 우습게 여기다

14

△ **unbelievable**
형 믿을 수 없는
유 incredible 놀라운,
믿어지지 않는
반 believable 믿을 수 있는

A 주어진 뜻을 잘 읽고, 빈칸에 해당하는 단어나 구를 쓰세요.

1. not beautiful, unattractive → u_____
2. to say sorry for something → a_____
3. to think you are better than someone → I_____
4. not old → n_____
5. to receive, to allow → a_____
6. to return → t_____
7. the number of years that a person has lived → a_____
8. to keep away from something → a_____
9. the word that you use when you ask for a reason → w_____
10. to identify from a past experience → r_____

B 다음 장면에 어울리는 단어를 넣어 문장을 완성하세요.

| explain | unbelievable | Whenever | behave |

1. _____ I see the twins, Mike and Mark, it's _____ that they are exactly the same.

2. Can you _____ how to distinguish them?

3. They _____ differently. Mike is calm, and Mark is active.

C 문장을 읽고, 빈칸에 알맞은 뜻을 쓴 후 해당하는 것을 선으로 연결하세요.

accept

Go!

- 동 인정하다 •
- 동 받아들이다 •
- 동 수락하다 •

- • She accepted his present.
  그녀는 그의 선물을 _____.

- • He accepted that it was his fault.
  그는 그것이 그의 잘못이라고 _____.

- • I will accept your request.
  나는 너의 요청을 _____ 것이다.

D 문장을 읽고, 빈칸에 알맞은 단어를 쓰세요.

1. Do you want to know what my _____ roommate looks like?
   내 새 룸메이트가 어떻게 생겼는지 알고 싶니?

2. He is _____ . 그는 못생겼어.

3. He looks older than his _____ . 그는 그의 나이보다 더 들어 보이지.

4. I didn't _____ him when I passed him on my way to school.
   나는 학교 가는 길에 그를 지나쳤을 때 그를 못 알아봤어.

5. Do you know _____ people don't like him? 왜 사람들이 그를 싫어하는지 아니?

6. I will _____ to you. 내가 너에게 설명할게.

7. Because he _____ badly. 왜냐하면 그가 나쁘게 행동하기 때문이야.

8. He _____ _____ _____ others. 그는 다른 사람들을 업신여겨.

9. So people _____ him. 그래서 사람들은 그를 피하지.

10. He never _____ . 그는 절대로 사과하지 않아.

11. He doesn't _____ any advice. 그는 어떠한 충고도 받아들이지 않아.

12. _____ I try to talk to him, he just ignores me.
    내가 그에게 말을 하려고 할 때마다, 그는 그냥 나를 무시해.

13. His behavior is _____ . 그의 행동은 참 놀라워.

14. I wish I could _____ _____ time to when I didn't know him.
    나는 그를 몰랐던 때로 시간을 되돌리고 싶어.

Turn Back Time

Ted _____ very rudely to his parents and friends when he was 7.

One day, something _____ happened to him.

When he looked in the mirror, he looked older than the other boys his _____.

"Oh, no! I'm so ug_____! I look like an old man."

Ted was sad, so he av_____ going outside. Ted regretted his bad behavior.

_____ he behaved well, he became younger.

Good behavior _____ _____ time.

"Ted, _____ don't you go outside and play with your friends?" Mom asked.

Ted went outside. His friends didn't _____ him.

"Who are you? Are you _____?"

"No, I'm not new. I'm Ted." Ted _____ what had happened to him.

They were surprised and felt sorry for him. Ted ap_____ to his friends.

"I'm sorry for hurting you. I _____ _____ _____ you before."

Ted's friends ac_____ his apology and played with him.

Ted thought, "I will be a better person from now on."

Word Box

why · apologized · accepted · unbelievable · ugly · behaved · looked down on · turned back · avoided · age · new · explained · recognize · Whenever

Unit 5
Space

✪ 초등 기본어휘 ◯ 중등 기본어휘 △ 확장어휘

1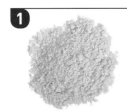
✪ **fine**
형 (알갱이가) 미세한, 가는, 좋은
명 벌금
❍ fine dust 미세한 먼지

2
✪ **moon**
명 달
❍ full moon 보름달
❍ half moon 반달
❍ new moon 초승달

3
✪ **near**
형 가까운
전 ~에서 가까이
반 far 먼
㋀ near here 이 근처에

4
✪ **circle**
동 회전하다
명 원
㋀ rotate 회전하다

5
◯ **data**
명 자료, 데이터
㋀ information 정보

6
◯ **deal**
동 다루다, 처리하다
(과거형 / 과거분사형 : dealt)
㋀ deal with a problem
문제를 처리하다

7
◯ **event**
명 사건, 행사
㋀ happening 사건
❍ charity event 자선 행사

8
◯ **launch**
동 발사하다, 쏘다

9
◯ **finally**
부 마침내, 최후로
㋀ in the end, eventually
결국, 마침내

10
◯ **history**
명 역사
㋀ chronicle 연대기
㋀ make history 역사에 남을
만한 일을 하다

11
◯ **astronaut**
명 우주비행사
㋀ spaceman, spacewoman
우주비행사

12
△ **alarm**
명 경보기, 자명종
동 놀라게 하다
❍ burglar alarm 도난 경보기

13
△ **footprint**
명 발자국
㋀ leave footprints in the
snow 눈에 발자국을 남기다

14
△ **spacecraft**
명 우주선
㋀ spaceship 우주선

A 주어진 뜻을 잘 읽고, 빈칸에 해당하는 단어를 쓰세요.

1. a mark that your foot leaves → f_____
2. a thing that makes a loud noise to wake you up → a_____
3. a rocket that travels in space → s_____
4. to solve or handle a problem → d_____
5. information on a computer → d_____
6. a person who travels in space → a_____
7. to send a rocket into the sky → l_____
8. the round thing that you can see in the sky at night → m_____
9. very small, very thin → f_____
10. to move around something; a round shape → c_____

B 연관되는 단어를 알아보고, 빈칸에 영어 또는 우리말 뜻을 쓰세요.

make ☐
역사에 남을 일을 하다
~ _____ 몡 역사 = chronicle 몡 _____

a sporting ☐
스포츠 행사
~ _____ 몡 사건, 행사 = _____ 몡 사건

☐, they got married.
마침내 그들은 결혼했다.
~ _____ 부 마침내, 최후로 = _____ 부 결국, 마침내

in the ☐ future
가까운 장래에
~ _____ 형 가까운 ↔ _____ 형 먼

C 빈칸에 알맞은 단어를 쓰고, 사다리를 타고 내려가 정답을 확인하세요.

1.
The moon _____ the Earth.

2.
I want to be an _____ .

3.
I turned off the _____ .

4.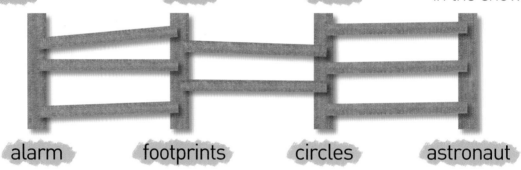
There are _____ in the snow.

alarm   footprints   circles   astronaut

D 문장을 읽고, 빈칸에 알맞은 단어를 쓰세요.

1. We will be able to travel to different planets in the _____ future.
   우리는 가까운 미래에 다른 행성들을 여행할 수 있을 것이다.

2. Scientists made a _____ .   과학자들은 우주선을 만들었다.

3. It was _____ into space.   그것은 우주로 발사되었다.

4. It was such a big _____ .   그것은 매우 큰 사건이었다.

5. Astronauts landed on the _____ .   우주비행사들이 달에 착륙했다.

6. They collected _____ there.   그들은 그곳에서 자료를 수집했다.

7. One day, _____ dust got into the computer.
   어느 날, 미세한 먼지가 컴퓨터 안으로 들어갔다.

8. They _____ with the problem calmly.   그들은 그 문제를 침착하게 해결했다.

9. _____ , they came back to Earth.   마침내, 그들은 지구로 돌아왔다.

10. They made _____ .   그들은 역사에 남을 일을 했다.

 빈칸에 알맞은 단어를 단어 박스에서 찾아 넣어 이야기를 완성하세요.

From the Earth to the Moon

Apollo 11 was an American _____.

Three as_____ were aboard *Apollo 11* in July 1969

They were on a mission to explore the _____.

Many people gathered _____ the space center.

Millions watched the _____ on television.

A rocket carrying *Apollo 11* was _____.

Apollo 11 _____ the Earth and then flew to the moon.

The _____ went off while landing on the moon.

There was trouble with the computer da_____.

But the astronauts _____ with the problem calmly.

They f_____y landed on the moon.

The astronauts stepped off *Apollo 11*.

The surface was covered with a fi_____ powder.

They left the first _____ on the moon.

The _____ of space travel to the moon began with *Apollo 11*.

Word Box

near   fine   dealt   footprints   circled

data   spacecraft   history   event   finally   launched

astronauts   alarm   moon

• Lesson 2 • Fly Me to Mars

⭐ 초등 기본어휘 ○ 중등 기본어휘 △ 확장어휘

1

⭐ hill
- 명 언덕, 낮은 산
- 유 mountain 산
- 구 go down the hill
  언덕을 내려가다

2

⭐ plate
- 명 접시
- 유 dish 접시
- ○ paper plate 종이 접시

3

⭐ holiday
- 명 휴일, 축제일, 휴가
- 유 vacation 휴가
- ○ national holiday 국경일

4

○ beg
- 동 부탁하다, 구걸하다
- 구 beg for money
  돈을 부탁하다

5

○ space
- 명 우주, 공간
- 유 universe 우주
- ○ space station 우주 정거장

6

○ discuss
- 동 토의하다, 토론하다
- 명 discussion 토론
- 유 debate 논쟁하다

7

○ suggest
- 동 제안하다, 추천하다, 암시하다
- 명 suggestion 제안, 의견
- 유 propose 제안하다

8

○ equipment
- 명 장비, 장치
- ○ camping equipment
  캠핑 장비

9

○ spacesuit
- 명 우주복

10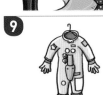

△ Mars
- 명 화성
- *cf.* Venus 금성, Jupiter 목성

11

△ alien
- 명 외계인, 외국인, 이방인
- 유 extraterrestrial
  외계인(= ET)

12

△ weird
- 형 이상한, 기이한
- 유 strange 이상한
- 반 normal 평범한

13

△ satellite
- 명 위성, 인공위성
- 구 launch a satellite
  인공위성을 발사하다

14

△ telescope
- 명 망원경
- 구 look through a telescope
  망원경으로 보다

A 주어진 뜻을 잘 읽고, 빈칸에 해당하는 단어를 쓰세요.

1. to talk about an issue with other people → d_____
2. to ask for something → b_____
3. a dish that you put food on → p_____
4. a period of time when you do not go to work or school → h_____
5. the area where stars are → s_____
6. the fourth planet in the solar system → M_____
7. a creature that lives on another planet → a_____
8. to tell someone your idea → s_____
9. the clothes that you wear in space → s_____
10. strange, not normal → w_____

B 다음 장면에 어울리는 단어를 넣어 문장을 완성하세요.

| hill | equipment | satellite | telescope |

1. They were sitting on the _____ at night. They saw something sparkling in the sky. "What is that?"
2. "I don't know. We need some _____."
3. They brought a _____ and watched it.
4. "It's a _____!"

C 문장을 읽고, 빈칸에 알맞은 뜻을 쓴 후 해당하는 것을 선으로 연결하세요.

(동) 제안하다 •

(동) 암시하다 •

suggest

Go!

(동) 추천하다 •

• His letter suggests that he loves her.
그의 편지는 그가 그녀를 사랑하는 것을 _____.

• Can you suggest a good book?
좋은 책 하나 _____?

• He suggests going to the party.
그는 파티에 가고 _____.

D 문장을 읽고, 빈칸에 알맞은 단어를 쓰세요.

1. Mark and I went on a picnic during the _____.   마크와 나는 휴일에 소풍을 갔다.

2. We went up the _____.   우리는 언덕에 올랐다.

3. We ate two _____ of sandwiches.   우리는 샌드위치 두 접시를 먹었다.

4. He _____ for more sandwiches.   그는 샌드위치를 좀 더 부탁했다.

5. After lunch, we _____ a problem.   점심을 먹은 후에 우리는 토론을 했다.

6. The topic was _____ exploration.   주제는 우주 탐험이었다.

7. "What _____ do we need?"   "어떤 장치가 필요할까?"

8. "We need a _____ to see stars."   "우리는 별들을 보기 위해 망원경이 필요해."

9. "Also, we should wear _____."   "또한, 우리는 우주복을 입어야 해."

10. "Did you see the _____ picture yesterday?"   "어제 위성 사진 봤니?"

11. "There was something on _____."   "화성에 무언가 있었어."

12. "Really? That is really _____."   "정말? 참 이상하네."

13. "Some say that it must be _____."   "몇몇 사람들은 그것이 외계인들이 틀림없다고 말해."

14. "They _____ that we prepare to meet them."
"그들은 우리가 그들을 만날 준비를 해야 한다고 제안했어."

 빈칸에 알맞은 단어를 단어 박스에서 찾아 넣어 이야기를 완성하세요.

Fly Me to Mars

Ted is really into stories about sp_____.

He hopes to meet _____.

But everybody laughs at his _____ ideas.

One day, a girl named Tara came to Ted.

She su_____ spending the summer _____ in space.

They _____ their plans for the space trip.

"We need _____, food, and a camera."

They get all the _____ ready for the trip.

"We're ready! Let's go." They go up the hi_____.

They look up at the sky through a _____.

A shooting star falls, and Tara says, "Now!"

Ted turns on the sa_____ radio.

Somebody talks to them. "I'm Sevi from _____."

Ted and Tara _____ her, "Can you fly us to Mars?"

The UFO is like a flying _____. It lands on the hill.

Ted and Tara get in the UFO and wave goodbye to the Earth.

Word Box

plate   discuss   satellite   Mars   beg

hill   spacesuits   suggests   holiday   weird

equipment   aliens   space   telescope

Unit 6
The Ocean

• Lesson 1 • *The Life of a Salmon*

★ 초등 기본어휘 ◇ 중등 기본어휘 ▲ 확장어휘

1
★ **rock**
- 명 바위
- 동 흔들다
- 유 stone 돌

2
★ **salt**
- 명 소금
- 형 소금이 든, 소금 맛이 나는
- 동 소금을 치다
- 구 in salt 소금을 친, 소금에 절인

3
◇ **fail**
- 동 실패하다
- 명 failure 실패
- 반 succeed 성공하다

4
◇ **male**
- 형 남성의, 수컷의
- 명 남성, 수컷
- 유 masculine 남성의

5
◇ **adult**
- 명 어른
- 형 어른의
- 유 grown-up 어른

6
◇ **enter**
- 동 ~에 들어가다, 입학하다
- 명 entrance 입구, 입학
- 반 exit 나가다; 출구

7
◇ **female**
- 형 여성의, 암컷의
- 명 여성, 암컷
- 유 feminine 여성의

8
◇ **return**
- 동 되돌아가다, 돌려주다
- 유 come back 돌아오다
- 구 return home 귀가하다

9
◇ **stream**
- 명 시내, 개울
- 동 흐르다
- 유 river 강
- 유 flow 흐르다

10
◇ **several**
- 형 몇몇의
- 유 a few 조금의, 몇몇의
- 구 for several years 몇 년 동안

11
◇ **survive**
- 동 살아남다, 생존하다
- 명 survival 생존

12
▲ **salmon**
- 명 연어
- ❍ smoked salmon 훈제 연어

13
▲ **instinct**
- 명 본능, 타고난 소질
- 구 by instinct 본능적으로

14
▲ **migration**
- 명 이주, 이동
- 동 migrate 이동하다
- ❍ bird migration 조류의 이주

A 주어진 뜻을 잘 읽고, 빈칸에 해당하는 단어를 쓰세요.

1. a woman or a girl ➜ f_____
2. a natural tendency that a person or an animal has ➜ i_____
3. a white powder used in cooking; not sweet ➜ s_____
4. to come back ➜ r_____
5. to remain alive ➜ s_____
6. a big fish with pink flesh ➜ s_____
7. a kind of stone ➜ r_____
8. to go inside ➜ e_____
9. a small river ➜ s_____
10. the movement of animals before winter ➜ m_____

B 연관되는 단어를 알아보고, 빈칸에 영어 또는 우리말 뜻을 쓰세요.

a [_____] lion
수컷 사자
~ _____ 형 남성의 ⬌ _____ 형 여성의

as an [_____]
어른으로서
~ _____ 명 어른 = grown-up 명 _____

[_____] an exam
시험에 떨어지다
~ _____ 동 실패하다 ⬌ _____ 동 성공하다

[_____] days ago
며칠 전에
~ _____ 형 몇몇의 = _____ 구 몇몇의

C 빈칸에 알맞은 단어를 쓰고, 사다리를 타고 내려가 정답을 확인하세요.

1. Could you pass me the _____?

2. I will _____ university soon.

3. _____ books are on the table.

4. I like smoked _____.

Several   salt   salmon   enter

D 문장을 읽고, 빈칸에 알맞은 단어를 쓰세요.

1. I went to a _____ with my family.   나는 가족들과 함께 개울에 갔다.

2. I found some fish between the _____.   나는 바위들 틈에서 물고기들을 발견했다.

3. We tried to catch them in a net but _____.
우리는 그물로 그것들을 잡으려고 했지만 실패했다.

4. I caught one small _____ fish.   나는 작은 수컷 물고기 한 마리를 잡았다.

5. My brother caught two large _____ fish.
내 남동생은 큰 암컷 물고기 두 마리를 잡았다.

6. Some fish have a special _____.   어떤 물고기들은 특별한 본능을 가지고 있다.

7. Have you heard about _____?   '이주'에 대해서 들어본 적이 있는가?

8. A young fish grows into an _____ fish.   어린 물고기는 어른 물고기로 자란다.

9. When it grows up, it _____ to the river.   그것은 자라면 강으로 돌아간다.

10. It struggles to _____ its journey.   그 여정에서 그것은 살아남기 위해 고군분투한다.

  빈칸에 알맞은 단어를 단어 박스에서 찾아 넣어 이야기를 완성하세요.

The Life of a Salmon

Here is a cold and clear st_____.

Some tiny baby s_____n swim in the fresh water.

They start their m_____ to the ocean.

Their bodies change to live in _____ water.

At last, they _____ the ocean.

They grow into _____ salmon in the ocean.

Some of them f_____ to live in the big ocean.

Only a few of them su_____ among the saltwater fish.

They leave the ocean after se_____ years.

They try to re_____ to their stream.

They have the _____ to go back home.

After arriving, the salmon lay eggs among the _____.

_____ salmon lay thousands of eggs. _____ salmon help them.

Soon after, both the female and male salmon die.

The life of a salmon begins and ends in the same place.

Word Box

Male rocks adult several salmon

instinct return Female fail salt

enter stream migration survive

•Lesson 2 • Pirates and Treasure

✪ 초등 기본어휘 ◯ 중등 기본어휘 ⬣ 확장어휘

1

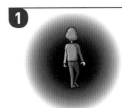

✪ **away**
㝅 떨어져, 사라져
㝅 run away 도망가다
㝅 get away 떠나다

2

✪ **ship**
명 배
㝅 boat 배, vessel (대형) 선박

3

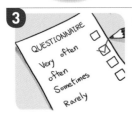

✪ **often**
㝅 종종, 자주
㝅 frequently 자주

4

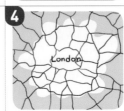

◯ **area**
명 지역, 범위
㝅 region 지역
❍ parking area 주차 구역

5

◯ **sweep**
동 (방·마당 등을) 쓸다,
쓸어버리다
(과거형 / 과거분사형: swept)
㝅 sweep away 쓸어내다

6

◯ **search**
동 찾다, 수색하다, 검색하다
명 조사, 수색
㝅 in search of ~을 찾아서

7

◯ **captain**
명 선장, 우두머리
㝅 commander 지휘관,
chief 우두머리

8

◯ **terrible**
형 끔찍한, 지독한

9

◯ **threaten**
동 위협하다, 협박하다
명 threat 위협, 협박
형 threatening 위협적인

10

◯ **treasure**
명 보물, 보배
㝅 jewels 보석

11

◯ **passenger**
명 승객, 여객
㝅 rider 타는 사람, 승객
❍ passenger plane 여객기

12

⬣ **cruise**
명 유람선 여행
동 순항하다
㝅 voyage 항해, 여행

13

⬣ **pirate**
명 해적
❍ pirate ship 해적선

14

⬣ **take over**
㝅 차지하다, 인수하다

A 주어진 뜻을 잘 읽고, 빈칸에 해당하는 단어나 구를 쓰세요.

1. a large boat → s_____
2. to gain something by force → t_____
3. a sailor who attacks other ships and steals things → p_____
4. expensive and valuable things → t_____
5. a trip on a ship or boat → c_____
6. to remove dust from the floor with a brush → s_____
7. a person who sails on a boat or takes a bus → p_____
8. the leader of a ship → c_____
9. very unpleasant or serious → t_____
10. many times, frequently → o_____

B 다음 장면에 어울리는 단어를 넣어 문장을 완성하세요.

| away | area | search | threatened |

1. I was walking around the downtown _____ at night.
2. Suddenly, a man appeared and _____ me.
3. He tried to _____ my pockets for money.
4. I was afraid and ran _____.

C 문장을 읽고, 빈칸에 알맞은 뜻을 쓴 후 해당하는 것을 선으로 연결하세요.

(동) 검색하다 •

(동) 수색하다 •

Go!

(동) 찾다 •

• He is <u>searching</u> for missing people in an accident.
그는 사고로 실종된 사람들을 _____.

• I <u>searched</u> for information on the Internet. 나는 인터넷에서 정보를 _____.

• The police <u>searched</u> the house.
경찰이 집을 _____.

D 문장을 읽고, 빈칸에 알맞은 단어를 쓰세요.

1. I have a lot of _____ sailing experiences. 나는 끔찍한 항해를 경험한 적이 많다.

2. I have sailed through a dangerous _____. 나는 위험한 지역을 항해한 적이 있다.

3. Sailors met _____ there frequently. 선원들은 그곳에서 해적들을 자주 만났다.

4. They _____ sailed there and took other _____.
그들은 종종 그곳에서 항해를 했고, 다른 배들을 빼앗았다.

5. They _____ _____ everything. 그들은 모든 걸 차지했다.

6. They _____ people. 그들은 사람들을 위협했다.

7. A month ago, I went on a _____. 한 달 전, 나는 유람선 여행을 했다.

8. Sailors _____ the deck of the ship. Suddenly, pirates appeared.
선원들은 배의 갑판을 쓸었다. 갑자기, 해적들이 나타났다.

9. All the _____ were scared. 모든 승객들은 두려워했다.

10. But the _____ couldn't do anything. 하지만 선장은 아무것도 할 수 없었다.

11. They started to _____ the ship. 그들은 배를 수색하기 시작했다.

12. Finally, they found the _____. 마침내, 그들은 보물을 찾았다.

13. They got _____ with it. 그들은 그것을 가지고 떠나가 버렸다.

 빈칸에 알맞은 단어를 단어 박스에서 찾아 넣어 이야기를 완성하세요.

Pirates and Treasure

Ted takes a _____ with his family.

Ted is very excited to sail the south ocean.

Ted asks the ca_____,

"Will we have a chance to see any pi_____?"

He answers, "Well, the west side is the dangerous ar_____.

Pirates _____ sail there. But we never go that far."

Ted has fun on the sh_____ in the calm ocean.

That night, a te_____ storm blows.

The ship is sw_____ to the west side of the ocean.

At last, the storm destroys the ship.

In the morning, scary pirates _____ _____ the ship.

Then they th_____ the pa_____.

Ted decides to save everyone and shouts at the pirates,

"There is a prince among the passengers. He has a big tr_____ chest

under his bed. You can take it!"

The pirates _____ for the treasure chest.

Ted and the other passengers take the pirates' ship and sail _____.

Word Box

threaten   area   pirates   away   take over

ship   passengers   captain   search   terrible

often   treasure   swept   cruise

Unit 7
Great Adventures

The Second to Reach the South Pole

✪ 초등 기본어휘 ◯ 중등 기본어휘 △ 확장어휘

1

✪ **a few**
구 (수) 약간, 조금
반 few 거의 없는
유 a little (양) 약간, 조금

2

✪ **run out of**
구 ~을 다 써버리다
유 use up 다 쓰다

3

◯ **shore**
명 해안, 물가
유 coast 해안
❍ sandy shore 모래 해변

4

◯ **suffer**
동 고통을 겪다, 견디다
명 sufferer 고통 받는 사람
구 suffer from ~으로 고생하다

5

◯ **attempt**
동 시도하다
명 시도
유 try 시도하다

6

◯ **prepare**
동 준비하다
유 get ready 준비하다
형 prepared 준비가 된

7

◯ **succeed**
동 성공하다
명 success 성공
형 successful 성공적인
반 fail 실패하다

8

◯ **vehicle**
명 탈것, 차
❍ motor vehicle 자동차

9

◯ **national**
형 국가의
명 nation 국가
명 nationality 국적

10

◯ **the English**
구 영국인들
형명 English 잉글랜드의,
영국의; 영어

11

△ **polar**
형 북극의, 극지의
❍ polar bear 북극곰
❍ the polar star 북극성

12

△ **exhausted**
형 기진맥진한
동 exhaust 다 써버리다,
소진하다
유 use up 다 써버리다

13

△ **frostbite**
명 동상
동 동상을 입다
구 suffer from frostbite
동상에 걸리다

14

△ **expedition**
명 탐험(대), 원정(대)
유 journey 여행
구 go on an expedition
탐험을 떠나다

A 주어진 뜻을 잘 읽고, 빈칸에 해당하는 단어나 구를 쓰세요.

1. extremely tired → e_____
2. the land near the sea → s_____
3. the British people → t_____
4. near the North or South Pole → p_____
5. connected to a nation → n_____
6. to be in pain → s_____
7. skin damage due to extreme cold → f_____
8. to get ready → p_____
9. something that carries you
   from one place to another → v_____
10. a long journey for a special reason → e_____

B 연관되는 단어를 알아보고, 빈칸에 영어 또는 우리말 뜻을 쓰세요.

[_____] in business
사업에 성공하다
~ _____ 동 성공하다 ↔ _____ 동 실패하다

[__][__][_____] cash
현금이 다 떨어지다
~ _____ 구 다 써버리다 = use up _____ 구 _____

He has [__][__] friends.
그는 친구가 약간 있다.
~ _____ 구 (수) 약간, 조금 → _____ 구 (양) 약간, 조금

[_____] to solve the problem
그 문제를 풀려고 시도하다
~ _____ 동 시도하다 = _____ 동 시도하다

C 빈칸에 알맞은 단어를 쓰고, 사다리를 타고 내려가 정답을 확인하세요.

1. He bought a new _____.

2. There are _____ eggs in the basket.

3. She went on an _____ through the jungle.

4. He was _____ after running.

expedition   vehicle   a few   exhausted

D 문장을 읽고, 빈칸에 알맞은 단어를 쓰세요.

1. I _____ at exploring the North Pole.   나는 북극을 탐험하는 데 성공했다.

2. On the first day, I was on the _____.   탐험 첫날, 나는 해안가에 있었다.

3. My car wouldn't start, so I _____ to fix it.
   내 차가 시동이 안 걸려서, 나는 그것을 고치려고 시도했다.

4. The reason was that it had _____ _____ _____ gas.
   가스가 떨어진 게 이유였다.

5. Luckily, _____ _____ helped me.   다행히, 영국 사람들이 나를 도와줬다.

6. Also, I _____ from the cold weather.   또한, 나는 추운 날씨 때문에 고생했다.

7. I _____ warm clothes.   나는 따뜻한 옷들을 준비했다.

8. So I didn't get _____.   그래서 동상에 걸리지 않았다.

9. I saw _____ bears resting on the ice.   나는 얼음 위에서 쉬고 있는 북극곰들을 보았다.

10. On the last day, I put our _____ flag there and came back.
    마지막 날, 나는 그곳에 우리 국기를 꽂고 돌아왔다.

 빈칸에 알맞은 단어를 단어 박스에서 찾아 넣어 이야기를 완성하세요.

The Second to Reach the South Pole

The _____ adventure began in the nineteenth century.

Many e_____ had tried to reach the South Pole before 1912.

But nobody suc_____ at getting to the South Pole.

Robert Scott was the leader of the English expedition.

His expedition at_____ to be the first to get to the South Pole.

They set up a base camp on the sh_____.

They carefully pr_____ the expedition.

They took sled dogs, ponies, and _____.

When they arrived at the South Pole, the Norwegian* flag was flying.

The Norwegians reached the South Pole 5 weeks before _____

_____.

They were very disappointed and _____.

They _____ from the bad weather on their way back.

They became ill and got _____.

They _____ _____ _____ food and died of hunger.

They were found _____ _____ kilometers from their base camp.

They failed but became _____ heroes.

* **Norwegian** 노르웨이의

Word Box

a few   attempted   national   expeditions   exhausted

prepared   succeeded   ran out of   frostbite   the English

shore   vehicles   polar   suffered

The Mystery of the Devil's Triangle

⭐ 초등 기본어휘 ⚪ 중등 기본어휘 🔺 확장어휘

1
⭐ **theater**
명 극장
⭕ movie theater 영화관

2
⭐ **daughter**
명 딸
반 son 아들
⭕ daughter-in-law 며느리

3
⭕ **triangle**
명 삼각형
cf. rectangle 직사각형
diamond 마름모

4
⭕ **draw into**
구 ~에 끌어들이다
동 draw 끌다, 잡아당기다
(과거형 : drew - 과거분사형 : drawn)

5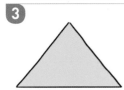
⚪ **press**
동 누르다, 밀다, 강요하다
명 언론
유 push 누르다

6
⚪ **reason**
명 이유
형 reasonable 이성적인, 이치에 맞는
유 cause 원인

7
⚪ **screen**
명 영화, 화면
⭕ computer screen 컴퓨터 화면

8
⚪ **situation**
명 상황, 처지
유 condition 상태
⭕ difficult situation 힘든 상황

9
⚪ **get worse**
구 악화되다
반 get better 좋아지다, 호전되다

10
🔺 **hero**
명 영웅
cf. heroine 여자 영웅, 여주인공
⭕ war hero 전쟁 영웅

11
🔺 **bubble**
명 거품
동 거품이 나다

12
🔺 **bacteria**
명 세균, 박테리아
(단수형 : bacterium)
유 germs 세균
⭕ bacteria-free 무균의

13
🔺 **submarine**
명 잠수함
⭕ nuclear submarine 핵 잠수함

14
🔺 **whirlpool**
명 소용돌이
유 vortex 소용돌이

A 주어진 뜻을 잘 읽고, 빈칸에 해당하는 단어나 구를 쓰세요.

1. to pull something in → d_____
2. a shape that has three sides → t_____
3. to push something → p_____
4. a man who does great things → h_____
5. a place that water spins very fast → w_____
6. something that travels underwater → s_____
7. a small ball of air within a liquid → b_____
8. a fact that explains why something happens → r_____
9. what you watch a movie on → s_____
10. a place where you watch movies or plays → t_____

B 다음 장면에 어울리는 단어나 구를 넣어 문장을 완성하세요.

| getting worse | situation | bacteria | daughter |

1. How is your _____?
2. Unfortunately, her _____ is not good.
3. Her condition is _____.
4. The doctor said that it is because of _____.

C 문장을 읽고, 빈칸에 알맞은 뜻을 쓴 후 해당하는 것을 선으로 연결하세요.

press

(동) 누르다 •

(동) 강요하다 •

Go!

(명) 언론 •

• The power of the press is strong.

_____의 힘은 강하다.

• He pressed for an answer.

그는 대답을 _____.

• I pressed a red button.

나는 빨간 단추를 _____.

D 문장을 읽고, 빈칸에 알맞은 단어를 쓰세요.

1. My family went to a movie _____ last Sunday.

   우리 가족은 지난 일요일에 영화관에 갔다.

2. The theater had a huge _____.   그 극장은 대형 화면을 갖추고 있었다.

3. The movie title was *The* _____.   영화 제목은 '소용돌이'였다.

4. It took place in the Bermuda _____.   배경은 버뮤다 삼각지였다.

5. The movie was about a _____.   영화는 한 영웅에 관한 이야기였다.

6. He explored the sea in a _____.   그는 잠수함을 타고 바다를 탐험했다.

7. It was _____ _____ deep water.   그것은 깊은 물속으로 빨려 들어갔다.

8. The water pressure _____ against his submarine.

   물의 압력이 그의 잠수함을 짓눌렀다.

9. The condition _____ _____.   상황은 더 악화되었다.

10. He dealt with this difficult _____.   그는 이 어려운 상황을 해결했다.

11. After watching the movie, my _____ asked me a question.

    영화를 본 후에, 딸이 나에게 질문을 했다.

12. "Why were there _____ in the deep underwater?"

    "왜 깊은 물속에 거품이 있었죠?"

13. I explained the _____.   나는 그 이유를 설명했다.

14. "_____ make oxygen."   "박테리아가 산소를 만들기 때문이란다."

 빈칸에 알맞은 단어를 단어 박스에서 찾아 넣어 이야기를 완성하세요.

The Mystery of the Devil's Triangle*

＊**the Devil's Triangle** 마의 삼각 지대(여러 비행기나 선박들이 알 수 없는 이유로 사라진 북대서양 서쪽 지역)

Ted watched a movie at the th_____.

It was an adventure film about the Devil's _____.

A scientist lost her da_____ in the Devil's Triangle.

Many ships and airplanes mysteriously disappeared there.

Ted says, "I want to discover the _____ they went missing."

At that moment, Ted falls into the _____.

Ted and a scientist get in a su_____ and go on an expedition.

Suddenly, a _____ forms near the Devil's Triangle.

The submarine is _____ _____ the hole.

Gas _____ up from the bottom of the sea.

Ted shouts, "It is _____ _____. The si_____ is very bad.

We are sinking because of the gas bubbles."

The scientist _____ a button.

Then, a lot of ba_____ come out and catch the gas bubbles.

They solve the mystery of the Devil's Triangle and become _____.

Word Box

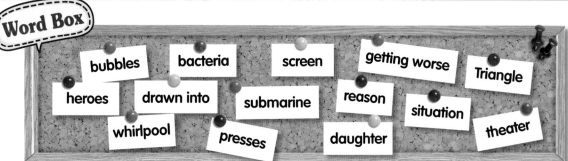

bubbles   bacteria   screen   getting worse   Triangle

heroes   drawn into   submarine   reason   situation

whirlpool   presses   daughter   theater

Unit 8
The Honor

★ 초등 기본어휘 ◇ 중등 기본어휘 ▲ 확장어휘

1
★ **corner**
명 구석, 모퉁이
구 take a corner 모퉁이를 돌다

2
◇ **cash**
명 현금, 돈
유 money 돈
구 pay in cash
현금으로 지불하다

3
◇ **honor**
동 존경하다, 영예를 주다
명 명예, 영광
반 dishonor 명예를 더럽히다;
불명예

4
◇ **since**
접 ~ 이래로, ~ 이후로

5
◇ **wealth**
명 부, 재산
형 wealthy 부유한
반 poverty 빈곤, 가난

6
◇ **consist**
동 (of) ~으로 이루어져 있다
유 be made up
~으로 이루어져 있다

7
◇ **physics**
명 물리학
명 physicist 물리학자

8
◇ **ceremony**
명 의식, 식
유 rite 의식
◐ religious ceremony
종교 의식

9
◇ **establish**
동 설립하다
유 set up 세우다, 건립하다

10
◇ **literature**
명 문학
◐ modern literature 현대
문학

11
◇ **anniversary**
명 기념일
◐ wedding anniversary
결혼기념일

12
◇ **international**
형 국제적인
유 global, worldwide
세계적인

13
▲ **more than**
구 ~보다 많은
반 less than ~보다 적은

14
▲ **be noted for**
구 ~으로 유명하다
유 be famous for
~으로 유명하다

A 주어진 뜻을 잘 읽고, 빈칸에 해당하는 단어나 구를 쓰세요.

1. the date of a special event → a_____
2. the celebration of a special event → c_____
3. to start or make → e_____
4. the scientific study of natural forces → p_____
5. to be well known for → b_____
6. bills and coins → c_____
7. from a moment in the past → s_____
8. written work such as novels and plays → l_____
9. to be made of → c_____
10. a point where two sides meet → c_____

B 연관되는 단어를 알아보고, 빈칸에 영어 또는 우리말 뜻을 쓰세요.

be in one's [_____]
~의 명예가 되다

명 명예 ↔ 명 불명예

[_____] **organization**
국제기구

형 국제적인 = **worldwide** 형 _____

[_____] [_____]
one year
일 년 이상

구 ~보다 많은 ↔ 구 ~보다 적은

gather [_____]
재산을 모으다

명 부, 재산 ↔ 명 빈곤

C 빈칸에 알맞은 단어를 쓰고, 사다리를 타고 내려가 정답을 확인하세요.

1.
Turn right at the _____.

2.
He is interested in _____.

3.
I don't have any _____.

4.
She attended the graduation _____.

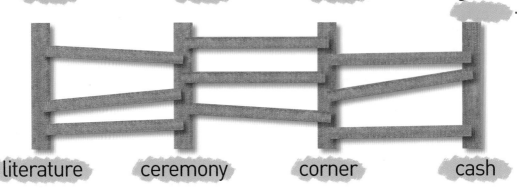

literature ceremony corner cash

D 문장을 읽고, 빈칸에 알맞은 단어를 쓰세요.

1. He is an _____ inventor. 그는 국제적인 발명가이다.

2. He received an _____ for being the scientist of the year.
그는 올해의 과학자라는 영예를 받았다.

3. _____ he majored in _____, he has invented many things.
물리학을 전공한 이후로, 그는 많은 것들을 발명했다.

4. His family _____ of six people. 그의 가족은 6명으로 구성되어 있다.

5. He is a millionaire, so it's difficult to imagine his _____.
그는 백만장자라서 그의 재산을 상상하기는 어렵다.

6. Also, he _____ _____ _____ his charity work.
또한, 그는 그의 자선 사업으로도 유명하다.

7. He _____ a school for the poor. 그는 가난한 사람들을 위한 학교를 설립했다.

8. It has _____ _____ 1,000 students. 그 학교에는 천 명이 넘는 학생들이 있다.

9. He gives scholarships to the best students on his wedding _____ every year. 그는 해마다 그의 결혼기념일에 최우수 학생들에게 장학금을 준다.

The Nobel Prize

The Nobel Prize is an in_____ award.

It awards people from all cor_____ of the world.

It _____ the people who did the best work in six different fields each year.

Three fields are in science. They are _____, chemistry[*], and medicine.

The others are _____, economic sciences, and work for world peace.

Alfred Nobel _____ the prize.

He was an inventor and businessman.

He _____ _____ _____ his invention of dynamite[*].

He left much of his _____ to establish the Nobel Prize.

The Nobel Prize has been awarded _____ 1901.

Every prize _____ of a diploma and a medal.

There are also ca_____ awards.

The awards ce_____ are held in Sweden and Norway.

They are on December 10, the _____ of Nobel's death.

_____ _____ 800 people have received prizes so far.

Who do you think the next Nobel Prize winner will be?

＊**chemistry** 화학   **dynamite** 다이너마이트

Word Box

consists   ceremonies   More than   since   literature

established   anniversary   is noted for   honors   corners

cash   physics   wealth   international

⭐ 초등 기본어휘 ⚪ 중등 기본어휘 🔺 확장어휘

1
⭐ **know**
통 알다, 구별하다, 알고 지내다
명 knowledge 지식
형 known 알려진

2
⭐ **correct**
형 옳은, 정확한
부 correctly 바르게, 정확하게
반 wrong 틀린, 잘못된

3
⭐ **question**
명 질문, 문제
통 질문하다
반 answer 대답; 대답하다

4
⚪ **chance**
명 기회, 운
유 opportunity 기회
구 by chance 우연히

5
⚪ **advance**
통 나아가다, 진보하다
명 전진, 진보
유 progress 진보하다; 진전

6
⚪ **mistake**
명 실수
구 make a mistake 실수하다

7
⚪ **confident**
형 자신 있는, 확신에 찬
명 confidence 자신(감), 신뢰
반 diffident 자신 없는

8
⚪ **everybody**
대 모든 사람, 누구든지
유 everyone 모든 사람

9
⚪ **dictionary**
명 사전

10
⚪ **competition**
명 경쟁, 대회
통 compete 경쟁하다
명 competitor 경쟁자

11
⚪ **participate**
통 (in) 참가하다, 참여하다
명 participant 참가자
유 take part (in) ~에 참여하다

12
⚪ **break wind**
구 방귀를 뀌다

13
🔺 **bloat**
통 부풀다, 더부룩하다
유 swell 부풀다
형 bloated 부푼
구 feel bloated 속이 더부룩하다

14
🔺 **giggle**
통 낄낄 웃다
유 laugh 웃다

A 주어진 뜻을 잘 읽고, 빈칸에 해당하는 단어나 구를 쓰세요.

1. a sentence in which one asks something   → q_____
2. to pass gas   → b_____
3. right, exact   → c_____
4. to be aware of, to understand   → k_____
5. a book of words and their meanings   → d_____
6. to swell, to increase in volume   → b_____
7. to take part in   → p_____
8. the possibility that something might happen   → c_____
9. to develop or improve   → a_____
10. all people   → e_____

B 다음 장면에 어울리는 단어를 넣어 문장을 완성하세요.

giggled	mistake	confident	competition

1. He took part in the piano _____.
2. He was very _____.
3. During the concert, he made a _____.
4. The audience _____.

C 문장을 읽고, 빈칸에 알맞은 뜻을 쓴 후 해당하는 것을 선으로 연결하세요.

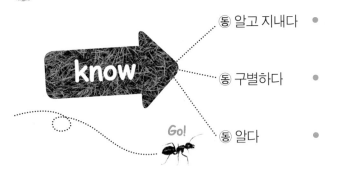

(동) 알고 지내다 •

(동) 구별하다 •

Go!

(동) 알다 •

• I **know** him well.
나는 그와 잘 _____.

• I already **know** the answer.
나는 정답을 이미 _____.

• I **know** right from wrong.
나는 옳고 그름을 _____.

D 문장을 읽고, 빈칸에 알맞은 단어를 쓰세요.

1. "I ate a lot last night, so I felt _____." "난 어젯밤에 너무 많이 먹어서 속이 더부룩했어."

2. "I studied all night because of the _____." "대회 때문에 밤새 공부했거든."

3. "As you know, I _____ to the final." "너도 알다시피 내가 결승전에 진출했잖아."

4. "Now, I regret that I _____ in it." "지금은 대회에 참가한 걸 후회해."

5. "Why? _____ is supporting you." "왜? 모두들 너를 응원하고 있어."

6. "Also, it is a good _____ for you." "또한 이것은 너에게 좋은 기회잖아."

7. "But I'm afraid of making a _____." "하지만 난 실수를 할까봐 두려워."

8. "What if I _____ _____ during the contest?"
"만약에 대회 동안에 방귀라도 뀌면 어떡하지?"

9. "Don't worry about it," I _____. "걱정하지 마." 나는 낄낄 웃었다.

10. "Anyway, I have a _____ for you." "그런데, 나 너에게 질문할 게 하나 있어."

11. "Do you _____ what this word means?" "이 단어의 의미가 무엇인지 아니?"

12. "Let me see. I don't think the spelling is _____."
"어디 보자. 내 생각엔 철자가 정확하지 않은 것 같아."

13. "I will look it up in the _____." "내가 사전을 찾아볼게."

14. "I am not _____ enough to say whether it is correct or not."
"그게 맞는지 아닌지 말하기에는 자신이 없네."

The Funny Winner

Ted _____ many words and likes to find the meanings of difficult words.

Every day, he reads many books and the _____.

One day, he _____ in a spelling bee.*

Ted and a girl _____ to the final round.

The girl looks very smart and _____.

She says, "I will be the winner of this com_____."

Almost _____ expects her to win.

But she gets confused and makes a _____.

The host says, "Now it's your ch_____, Ted."

He asks the final _____ to Ted.

Ted feels bl_____ and can't answer.

"Well, the answer is ... The answer is ..."

Suddenly, he _____ _____ very loudly.

People start to _____, so Ted feels nervous.

"Ha-ha-ha. The answer is b-l-i-z-z-a-r-d.*"

"Wow, that's cor_____! You are the funny winner of the spelling bee."

＊**spelling bee** 철자법 대회 **blizzard** 눈보라

Word Box

question　knows　everybody　breaks wind　bloated

advance　chance　confident　correct

dictionary　giggle　mistake　participates　competition

Unit 9
Step Back in Time

⭐ 초등 기본어휘 ⭕ 중등 기본어휘 🔺 확장어휘

1
⭐ **bath**
명 목욕, 욕조
동 bathe 씻다
구 take a bath 목욕하다

2
⭐ **shop**
명 가게
동 (물건을) 사다
유 store 가게, 점포

3
⭐ **mountain**
명 산
형 mountainous 산이 많은

4
⭕ **bury**
동 묻다
(과거형 / 과거분사형 : buried)
명 burial 매장

5
⭕ **remain**
동 남다, 여전히 ~이다
명 remains 나머지, 유적
유 stay 머무르다

6
⭕ **disaster**
명 재난
유 tragedy 비극
⭕ disaster film 재난 영화

7
⭕ **preserve**
동 보존하다, 지키다
명 preservation 보존
유 conserve 보존하다

8
⭕ **ash**
명 재, 화산재
⭕ ash heap 잿더미

9
🔺 **erupt**
동 분출하다, 폭발하다
명 eruption 분출, 폭발
유 blow up 폭발하다

10
🔺 **later**
부 나중에
유 after 뒤에
반 earlier 미리, 일찍

11
🔺 **petrify**
동 석화하다, 돌이 되다
(과거형 / 과거분사형 : petrified)

12
🔺 **uncover**
동 밝히다, 알아내다
유 discover 발견하다
반 cover 숨기다

13
🔺 **volcano**
명 화산
⭕ active volcano 활화산

14
🔺 **archaeologist**
명 고고학자
명 archaeology 고고학

A 주어진 뜻을 잘 읽고, 빈칸에 해당하는 단어를 쓰세요.

1. a terrible accident → d_____
2. not to be destroyed, taken, or used up → r_____
3. a person who studies remains from the past → a_____
4. a large and high landform → m_____
5. washing your body → b_____
6. a place where you buy things → s_____
7. to put in the earth and to cover up → b_____
8. the grey powder of something burned → a_____
9. to turn something into stone → p_____
10. a mountain which has hot melted rock inside → v_____

B 연관되는 단어를 알아보고, 빈칸에 영어 또는 우리말 뜻을 쓰세요.

See you _____.
나중에 보자.　　　　　_____ 　　⟷ 　_____
　　　　　　　　　　　　　(부) 나중에　　　　　(부) 미리, 일찍

_____ the environment
환경을 보존하다　　　_____ 　　= 　conserve
　　　　　　　　　　　(동) 보존하다　　　　(동) _____

_____ a secret
비밀을 밝히다　　　　_____ 　　⟷ 　_____
　　　　　　　　　　　(동) 밝히다　　　　　(동) 숨기다

A volcano _____.
화산이 분출했다.　　　_____ 　　= 　_____
　　　　　　　　　　　(동) 분출하다　　　　(구) 폭발하다

C 빈칸에 알맞은 단어를 쓰고, 사다리를 타고 내려가 정답을 확인하세요.

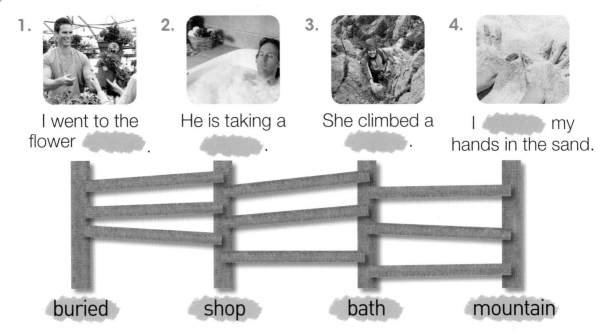

1. I went to the flower _____ .

2. He is taking a _____ .

3. She climbed a _____ .

4. I _____ my hands in the sand.

buried   shop   bath   mountain

D 문장을 읽고, 빈칸에 알맞은 단어를 쓰세요.

1. An _____ visited a town.   한 고고학자가 어떤 마을을 방문했다.

2. The town was covered with _____ .   그 마을은 재로 덮여 있었다.

3. The reason _____ a mystery.   그 이유는 수수께끼로 남아 있었다.

4. He saw a _____ not far from the town and thought it might be a _____ .   그는 마을에서 멀지 않은 곳에 있는 산을 보고 아마도 화산이었을 것이라고 생각했다.

5. It might have _____ in the past.   그 화산은 과거에 분출했을 것이다.

6. _____ , he came back to the town with some help.
나중에, 그는 일꾼들을 데리고 마을로 돌아왔다.

7. They found _____ buildings and people underground.
그들은 땅속에서 석화된 건물과 사람들을 발견했다.

8. The buildings were _____ well.   그 건물들은 잘 보존되어 있었다.

9. He thought, "It was a terrible _____ ."   '끔찍한 재난이었군.'이라고 그는 생각했다.

10. At last, he _____ the mystery of the town.
마침내, 그는 그 마을의 수수께끼를 밝혀냈다.

빈칸에 알맞은 단어를 단어 박스에서 찾아 넣어 이야기를 완성하세요.

The Lost City of Pompeii*

Pompeii was an ancient Roman city.

It had a large market, a theater,

and many _____.

Many people enjoyed taking _____ and relaxing in Pompeii.

A _____ and the sea were near the city.

One day, the mountain _____. In other words, a _____ erupted.

Gas, _____, and rocks covered the city.

The people of the ancient city of Pompeii did not have a chance to escape.

Pompeii was quickly bu_____ by the volcanic eruption.*

The _____ of Pompeii was forgotten.

1,700 years _____, people found the lost city of Pompeii.

They _____ some Roman paintings.

_____ came and dug up the remains of the city.

A lot of _____ bodies of people and animals were discovered.

They were pr_____ well by the ash and mud.

Surprisingly, some buildings, houses, and streets _____.

Now we can visit Pompeii and learn about life in ancient Rome.

＊**Pompeii** 폼페이(이탈리아의 고대 도시) **volcanic eruption** 화산 분출

Word Box

mountain　baths　volcano　remained　disaster
uncovered　Archaeologists　preserved　buried　later　erupted
petrified　shops　ash

• Lesson 2 • The Stone Age

1
✪ **clock**
명 시계
❍ alarm clock 자명종
❍ cuckoo clock 뻐꾸기시계

2
✪ **knife**
명 칼
유 blade 칼날
유 cutter 베는 도구

3
✪ **point**
동 가리키다
명 뾰족한 끝
구 point at ~을 가리키다

4
◐ **raw**
형 날것의
유 uncooked 익히지 않은
구 in the raw 날것 그대로

5
◐ **set**
동 (기계 등을) 조정하다, 놓다, 두다
명 한 벌, 한 세트

6
◐ **edge**
명 끝, 가장자리
구 on the edge of ~의 모서리에
구 on edge 초조하여, 불안하여

7
◐ **spin**
동 돌다, 회전하다, 돌리다
(과거형 / 과거분사형: spun)

8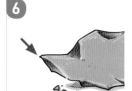
◐ **tool**
명 도구
유 instrument 도구

9
◐ **faint**
동 기절하다
유 pass out 기절하다
유 black out 의식을 잃다

10
◐ **sharp**
형 날카로운
부 sharply 날카롭게
반 blunt 무딘, 뭉툭한

11
◐ **create**
동 창조하다, 만들다
명 creation 창조
유 make 만들다

12
◐ **wonder**
동 궁금해하다, 놀라다
형 놀라운
구 no wonder 당연하다, 놀랄 것 없다

13
◐ **surround**
동 둘러싸다
유 encircle 에워싸다

14
◭ **Stone Age**
명 석기 시대
❍ Old Stone Age 구석기 시대
❍ New Stone Age 신석기 시대

A 주어진 뜻을 잘 읽고, 빈칸에 해당하는 단어를 쓰세요.

1. to make something new → c_____
2. to hold up your index finger toward something → p_____
3. to arrange or fix something → s_____
4. to move round rapidly → s_____
5. to be amazed at something → w_____
6. to black out → f_____
7. a thing used to make or repair something → t_____
8. a device that is used to tell the time → c_____
9. natural, uncooked → r_____
10. to enclose on all sides → s_____

B 다음 장면에 어울리는 단어를 넣어 문장을 완성하세요.

| knives | sharp | Stone Age | edges |

1. People used things made of stone in the _____.
2. Nowadays, we use _____, forks, and scissors.
3. We should be careful when we use these _____ things.
4. You can cut your finger easily on their sharp and pointy _____.

C 문장을 읽고, 빈칸에 알맞은 뜻을 쓴 후 해당하는 것을 선으로 연결하세요.

set

Go!

- 통 놓다 •
- 통 조정하다, 맞추다 •
- 명 한 벌, 한 세트 •

- • I bought a chess <u>set</u>.
  나는 체스 _____를 샀다.
- • He <u>set</u> a cup on the table.
  그는 컵을 탁자 위에 _____.
- • She <u>set</u> a dial on the oven.
  그녀는 오븐의 다이얼을 _____.

D 문장을 읽고, 빈칸에 알맞은 단어를 쓰세요.

1. My alarm _____ didn't go off, so I overslept.   나는 자명종이 울리지 않아 늦잠을 잤다.

2. The small hand on the clock was _____ to 9 by the time I got to school.   내가 학교에 도착했을 때 시침이 9시를 가리키고 있었다.

3. My friends were learning about the _____ _____.
   친구들은 석기 시대에 대해 배우고 있었다.

4. In this period, people used stone as a _____.
   이 시대에는 사람들이 도구로 돌을 사용했다.

5. _____ were also made of stone.   칼도 역시 돌로 만들어졌다.

6. They ground stones and made them _____.   그들은 돌을 갈아서 날카롭게 만들었다.

7. People used the stones' sharp _____.   사람들은 돌의 날카로운 끝부분들을 사용했다.

8. First, they _____ a trap to hunt animals.
   먼저, 그들은 동물을 사냥하려고 덫을 놓았다.

9. After finding an animal, they _____ it.   동물을 발견한 후에 그들은 그것을 둘러쌌다.

10. They hit the animal with their weapons and made it _____.
    그들은 자신들의 무기로 그 동물을 때려서 기절시켰다.

11. The women _____ a spinning wheels at home.   여자들은 집에서 물레를 돌렸다.

12. They ate _____ meat.   그들은 날고기를 먹었다.

13. That was no _____ at that time.   그것은 그 당시에 놀라운 일이 아니었다.

14. Because fire hadn't been _____.   왜냐하면 불이 만들어지지 않았었기 때문이다.

빈칸에 알맞은 단어를 단어 박스에서 찾아 넣어 이야기를 완성하세요.

The Stone Age

Ted looks at the _____ in the morning.

It stops and _____ at 12.

He tries to _____ the clock.

But it suddenly sp_____ back.

Ted feels dizzy and _____.

When he wakes up, he is su_____ by people.

A woman smiles,

"Don't worry. We will take care of you."

They look like people from the St_____ _____

because they are wearing animal skins.

The men go hunting with stone _____.

But the stone tools are not sh_____.

Ted breaks and sharpens the _____ of a stone.

It becomes a sharp stone _____.

People look at Ted and _____ where he came from.

People hunt a bear and cut meat with stone knives.

Ted says, "Wait! Don't eat _____ meat."

Ted rubs two stones together and makes a fire.

People shout, "You cr_____ fire! You're our king!"

Word Box

faints   tools   created   wonder   edge

clock   Stone Age   surrounded   set   knife

sharp   spins   points   raw

Unit 10
World Landmark

• Lesson 1 • *The Leaning Tower of Pisa*

★ 초등 기본어휘 ◇ 중등 기본어휘 △ 확장어휘

1
★ **finish**
동 끝내다
유 complete 완성하다, 끝내다

2
◇ **bell**
명 종
구 ring a bell 종을 울리다

3
◇ **lean**
동 기울다, 기대다
유 recline 기대다
구 lean against ~에 기대다

4
◇ **cease**
동 중단하다, 그만두다
유 stop 멈추다
유 halt 중지하다

5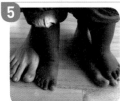
◇ **belong**
동 속하다
구 belong to ~의 소유이다

6
◇ **degree**
명 정도, (온도·각도) 도, 학위
➡ 45 degrees 45도

7
◇ **effort**
명 노력
구 make an effort 노력하다

8
◇ **vertical**
형 수직의, 세로의
반 horizontal 수평의, 가로의

9
◇ **foundation**
명 기반, 기초
동 found 기초를 세우다, 설립하다

10
◇ **remarkable**
형 놀랄 만한, 뛰어난
부 remarkably 두드러지게
유 extraordinary 뛰어난

11
◇ **construction**
명 건설
동 construct 건설하다
반 destruction 파괴

12
◇ **even though**
접 비록 ~일지라도
유 even if 비록 ~일지라도

13
△ **marble**
명 대리석, 구슬

14
△ **unstable**
형 불안정한
반 stable 안정된

A 주어진 뜻을 잘 읽고, 빈칸에 해당하는 단어나 구를 쓰세요.

1. in spite of the fact that → e_____
2. trying to achieve something → e_____
3. surprising, outstanding → r_____
4. something made of metal and that makes a sound → b_____
5. the process of building → c_____
6. to be in a place or group → b_____
7. a unit of measurement for temperature → d_____
8. to stop → c_____
9. a type of stone used in buildings → m_____
10. the ground, the base → f_____

B 연관되는 단어를 알아보고, 빈칸에 영어 또는 우리말 뜻을 쓰세요.

_____ line
수직선
~ _____ 형 수직의 ⟷ _____ 형 수평의

_____ your
homework.
숙제를 끝내라.
~ _____ 동 끝내다 = complete 동 _____

an _____ situation
불안정한 상황
~ _____ 형 불안정한 ⟷ _____ 형 안정된

_____ against
the wall
벽에 기대다
~ _____ 동 기대다 = recline 동 _____

C 빈칸에 알맞은 단어를 쓰고, 사다리를 타고 내려가 정답을 확인하세요.

1.

The building is under _____.

2.

_____ she's old, she is really attractive.

3.

The floor is made of _____.

4.
Don't _____ on the door.

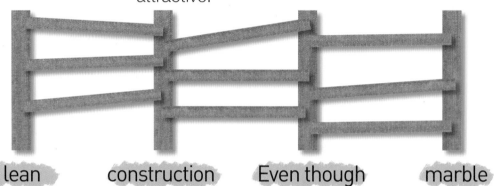

lean   construction   Even though   marble

D 문장을 읽고, 빈칸에 알맞은 단어를 쓰세요.

1. I have a master's _____ in architecture. 나는 건축학 석사 학위를 가지고 있다.

2. Now, I _____ to a big company. 현재, 나는 큰 회사에 속해 있다.

3. I designed a _____ building. 나는 놀랄 만한 건물을 하나 디자인했다.

4. It has a _____ structure. 그것은 수직적 구조를 가지고 있다.

5. It has a _____ hanging from the ceiling. 그것은 천장에 종이 달려 있다.

6. I haven't _____ building it yet. 나는 그것을 짓는 것을 아직 끝내지 못했다.

7. There was a problem with the _____. It was too weak.
   기반에 문제가 있었다. 너무 약했다.

8. So I _____ construction on the building. 그래서 나는 그 건물을 짓는 것을 중단했다.

9. I am making an _____ to handle it. 나는 그것을 해결하기 위해 노력 중이다.

10. But the situation is very _____. 하지만 상황이 매우 불안정하다.

빈칸에 알맞은 단어를 단어 박스에서 찾아 넣어 이야기를 완성하세요.

The Leaning Tower of Pisa*

The Leaning Tower of Pisa is a famous b_____ tower in the Italian city of Pisa.

The tower _____ to the church of Pisa.

It has 8 stories covered in white _____.

They began building the tower in 1173.

It was originally designed to be _____.

But it began to sink after co_____ on the third floor in 1178.

Why did the tower sink and _____?

The tower was built on weak, _____ ground.

The builders made an ef_____ to stop it from sinking.

After several attempts, they _____ building the tower for a century.

When the fo_____ became more stable, it was built again.

They _____ building the tower and added five more floors 200 years later.

It leans at an angle of about 3.99 _____ now and continues to sink slowly.

_____ _____ it leans, it looks attractive.

Many tourists visit this _____ tower and take pictures.

*the Leaning Tower of Pisa 피사의 사탑

Word Box

ceased   remarkable   foundation   construction   finished

lean   Even though   degrees   belongs   marble

effort   unstable   vertical   bell

Climbing a Bridge

🌟 초등 기본어휘 ◯ 중등 기본어휘 △ 확장어휘

1 🌟 **early**
🔵 일찍
🔴 late 늦게
🟩 early in the morning
아침 일찍

2 🌟 **bridge**
🟥 다리
⭕ suspension bridge 현수교
(케이블에 의해 지지되도록
만든 다리)

3 ◯ **rope**
🟥 밧줄
🟨 cord 끈
🟨 cable (굵은) 밧줄, 케이블

4 ◯ **shock**
🟦 충격을 주다
🟥 충격
🟩 shocked 충격을 받은
⭕ culture shock 문화 충격

5 ◯ **steep**
🟩 가파른, 경사가 급한

6 ◯ **tight**
🟩 단단한, 꽉 조이는, 곤란한
🔵 단단히, 꽉
🟦 tighten 죄다
⭕ tight knot 단단한 매듭

7 ◯ **beside**
🟪 ~ 옆에, ~ 곁에
🟨 next to ~ 바로 옆에

8 ◯ **neighbor**
🟥 이웃
🟨 neighborhood
이웃, 이웃 사람들

9 ◯ **on air**
🟩 방송 중에
🟩 put ~ on air ~을 방송하다

10 ◯ **walk across**
🟩 ~을 걸어서 건너다

11 △ **landmark**
🟥 중요 지형지물, 명소, 랜드마크,
획기적 사건

12 △ **guardrail**
🟥 (계단) 난간, 가드레일
🟦🟥 guard 지키다; 보호자

13 △ **mind one's step**
🟩 발걸음을 조심하다
🟨 watch one's step
조심하다, 조심해 걷다

14 △ **miss one's step**
🟩 발을 헛디디다
🟨 lose one's step
발을 잘못 디디다

A 주어진 뜻을 잘 읽고, 빈칸에 해당하는 단어나 구를 쓰세요.

1. next to something → b_____
2. a person who lives next door → n_____
3. the opposite of "late" → e_____
4. to surprise in an unpleasant way → s_____
5. rising or falling quickly → s_____
6. a thing that prevents people from falling over → g_____
7. to walk carefully → m_____
8. broadcasting on radio or television → o_____
9. a line that you use for tying knots → r_____
10. fixed firmly → t_____

B 다음 장면에 어울리는 단어나 구를 넣어 문장을 완성하세요.

landmark   walked across   Bridge   missed my step

1. I went to the Brooklyn [_____] when I traveled to the USA.
2. It is a [_____] in New York City.
3. I [_____] the bridge from Brooklyn to Manhattan.
4. I almost fell over because I [_____].

C 문장을 읽고, 빈칸에 알맞은 뜻을 쓴 후 해당하는 것을 선으로 연결하세요.

(형) 단단한　●

(형) 꽉 조이는　●

Go!

(형) 곤란한　●

● I'm going through a tight situation.
　나는 _____ 상황을 겪고 있는 중이다.

● This shirt is too tight for me.
　이 셔츠는 나에게 너무 _____.

● I made a tight knot.
　나는 _____ 매듭을 지었다.

D 문장을 읽고, 빈칸에 알맞은 단어를 쓰세요.

1. There is a very _____ mountain.　경사가 매우 급한 산이 있다.

2. There is also a beautiful river _____ it.　그 옆에는 또 아름다운 강이 있다.

3. It is a _____ in the town.　그것은 마을의 랜드마크이다.

4. It was put _____ _____.　이것은 방송에 나왔었다.

5. _____ in the morning, I left home to climb it.
　아침 일찍, 나는 그 산에 오르기 위해 집을 떠났다.

6. I took a backpack and _____.　나는 배낭과 밧줄을 챙겼다.

7. I wore thick clothes that were a little _____ for me.
　나는 나에게 조금 꽉 끼는 두꺼운 옷을 입었다.

8. I asked my _____ how to get there.　나는 그곳에 어떻게 가는지 내 이웃에게 물었다.

9. He said that I should cross the _____.　그는 내가 다리를 건너야 한다고 말했다.

10. At the bridge, there was a sign that read " _____ _____
_____ !"　다리에는 '걸음을 조심하시오!'라는 표지가 있었다.

11. I _____ _____ it.　나는 그것을 걸어서 건너갔다.

12. Suddenly, I _____ _____ _____.　갑자기, 나는 발을 헛디뎠다.

13. I was _____ and frightened.　나는 충격을 받았고 놀랐다.

14. Luckily, there was a _____, so I didn't fall over.
　다행히, 가드레일이 있어서 떨어지지는 않았다.

E 빈칸에 알맞은 단어를 단어 박스에서 찾아 넣어 이야기를 완성하세요.

Climbing a Bridge

Ted leaves home _____ in the morning.

He goes on a picnic with his _____ Sam.

Sam is good at climbing st_____ walls.

So people call him "Spider Sam."

They arrive at a wide river _____ a park.

There's a br_____ over the river.

It is narrow and made of _____.

They _____ _____ the bridge to get to the park.

When they reach the middle of the bridge,

Sam _____ _____ _____.

Ted is _____ and shouts,

"Watch out! _____ _____ _____!"

Sam hangs and dangles from the rope.

Ted shouts, "Hold on _____."

Sam moves up the g_____ and climbs back onto the bridge.

"Oh, this bridge is perfect for climbing on."

His brave act on the bridge is put _____ _____.

After that, the bridge becomes a famous _____ around the world.

Word Box

guardrail　steep　Mind your step　misses his step　shocked
tight　on air　beside　rope
neighbor　early　bridge　landmark　walk across

Unit 1

The Fortune
부

• Lesson 1 • **A Rich Boy**   p.10

Ⓐ 1. customer   2. year   3. homeless   4. mow
   5. court   6. week   7. charity   8. young
   9. dozen   10. blanket

Ⓑ

hire | a clerk ↔ hire 통 고용하다 | fire 통 해고하다
점원을 고용하다

without | a reason ↔ without 전 ~ 없어 | with 전 ~와 함께
이유 없이

make a | fortune ≡ fortune 명 재산, 부 | wealth 명 부
부자가 되다

come to | nothing ↔ nothing 대 아무것도 아닌 것 | everything 대 모든 것
(노력이) 수포로 돌아가다

Ⓒ 1. dozen   2. court   3. hire   4. week

Ⓓ 1. mowing   2. years   3. young   4. nothing
   5. fortune   6. customers 7. without   8. homeless
   9. blankets   10. charities

Ⓔ **A Rich Boy**   p.13

Ryan Ross is a 9-**year**-old boy who runs his own business.
When he was three years old, he sold 20 **dozen** fresh eggs.
He made about 50 dollars a **week**.
Later, he had a lawn-**mowing** business.
He was too **young** to mow lawns.
So he **hired** older kids to mow for 15 dollars an hour.
He charged his **customers** 20 dollars an hour.
He made 5 dollars an hour **without** doing any work.
After that, he made a **fortune** in his power-washing business.
Now, he has six buildings.
He has a hockey rink and a basketball **court**.
He also runs a **charity**.

He collects **blankets** to help the **homeless**.
His big dream is to buy his own hockey team.
He says, "**Nothing** is stopping me. What's stopping you?"

● 해석 ●
부자 소년
라이언 로스는 자신의 사업을 운영하는 9세 소년이다.
3세 때, 그는 20 다스의 신선한 계란을 팔았다.
그는 일주일에 약 50 달러를 벌었다.
나중에, 그는 잔디 깎는 사업을 했다.
그는 잔디를 깎기엔 너무 어렸다.
그래서 그는 한 시간에 15 달러를 주고 잔디를 깎을 나이가 더 많은 아이들을 고용했다.
그는 고객들에게 한 시간에 20 달러를 부과했다.
그는 아무 일도 하지 않고 한 시간에 5 달러를 벌었다.
그 후에, 그는 강력 세척사업으로 큰 돈을 벌었다.
지금 그는 6채의 건물을 가지고 있다.
그는 하키 링크와 농구장을 가지고 있다.
그는 또한 자선 단체도 운영하고 있다.
그는 집 없는 사람들을 돕기 위해서 담요들을 수집한다.
그의 큰 꿈은 자기 소유의 하키팀을 사는 것이다.
그는 말한다. "아무것도 나를 막을 수 없어요. 무엇이 당신을 막고 있나요?"

• Lesson 2 • **A Smart Invention** p.14

Ⓐ 1. trap   2. maybe   3. connect
   4. burglar   5. delivery   6. doorbell
   7. hesitate   8. make angry   9. weak
   10. run errands

Ⓑ 1. inventions   2. cell phone   3. earned   4. millionaire

Ⓒ
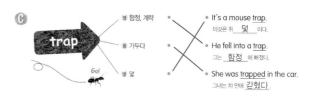

trap
명 함정, 계략
통 가두다
명 덫

• It's a mouse trap.
이것은 쥐 덫 이다.
• He fell into a trap.
그는 함정 에 빠졌다.
• She was trapped in the car.
그녀는 차 안에 갇혔다.

Ⓓ 1. millionaire   2. delivery   3. made, angry
   4. run errands   5. earn   6. burglar
   7. trap, connected 8. invention   9. weak
   10. cell phone   11. doorbell   12. hesitated
   13. Maybe

ⓔ A Smart Invention p.17

Ted's mom complains. "I've got some missing **deliveries**. **Maybe** somebody took them."

Every day, Ted hides and waits for the **burglar**.

One day, a tall man comes to his house.

He rings the **doorbell** to see if anyone is at home.

Then, he whistles and takes Ted's delivery.

Ted wants to **make** him **angry**.

He **connects** the doorbell to his **cell phone**.

The burglar comes back when Ted goes out to **run** some **errands**.

He rings the doorbell again, and Ted answers his cell phone.

Ted says, "I'm so old and **weak**. Can you come in and help me?"

The burglar **hesitates** a little but tries to steal things in the house.

"Oh, no!" The burglar is **trapped** in a net, and the police officers come.

The next morning, Ted's mom says, "Ted, you're in the newspaper."

People buy his smart **invention**.

He **earns** a lot of money and becomes a **millionaire**.

● 해석 ●
영리한 발명품

테드의 엄마는 불평한다. "배달물들이 사라져 버렸어. 아마도 누군가가 그것들을 가져갔나 봐."

매일, 테드는 숨어서 강도를 기다린다.

어느 날, 키가 큰 한 남자가 그의 집에 온다.

그는 집에 사람이 있는지 알아보기 위해 초인종을 누른다.

그런 다음, 그는 휘파람을 불고 테드의 배달물을 가져간다.

테드는 그를 약 올리고 싶다.

그는 초인종을 그의 휴대 전화에 연결한다.

테드가 심부름을 하러 외출했을 때, 강도가 또 온다.

그가 초인종을 다시 누르고, 테드가 그의 휴대 전화를 받는다.

테드가 말한다. "나는 너무 늙었고 약하다네. 들어와서 나를 좀 도와주겠나?"

강도는 조금 망설이지만, 집안의 물건을 훔치려고 한다.

"오, 안돼!" 강도는 그물 안에 갇히고, 경찰들이 온다.

다음날 아침, 테드의 엄마가 말한다. "테드, 네가 신문에 나왔구나."

사람들은 그의 영리한 발명품을 산다.

그는 많은 돈을 벌고 백만장자가 된다.

Unit 2
The Bat
박쥐

• Lesson 1 • **The Lives of Bats** p.18

ⓐ 1. raise 2. death 3. western 4. symbol
5. bounce 6. flap 7. sound 8. prey
9. bat 10. mammal

ⓑ
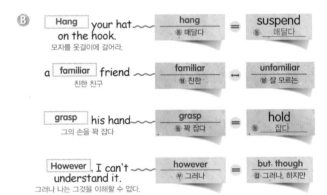

Hang your hat on the hook. 모자를 옷걸이에 걸어라.	hang ⑧ 매달다	=	suspend ⑧ 매달다
a familiar friend 친한 친구	familiar ⑱ 친한	↔	unfamiliar ⑲ 잘 모르는
grasp his hand 그의 손을 꽉 잡다	grasp ⑧ 꽉 잡다	=	hold ⑧ 잡다
However I can't understand it. 그러나 나는 그것을 이해할 수 없다.	however ⑮ 그러나	=	but, though ⑮ 그러나, 하지만

ⓒ 1. Western 2. sounds 3. prey 4. grasp

ⓓ 1. mammal 2. flap 3. hangs 4. bat
5. raised 6. familiar 7. bounced 8. symbol
9. death 10. However

ⓔ The Lives of Bats p.21

Bats are found almost everywhere in the world.

But people aren't **familiar** with them. What about you? Do you like bats?

They are the only **mammals** that can fly.

They can **flap** by spreading out their wings.

Many bats live in trees by **hanging** on the branches.

Some of them live in caves.

They are perfect places to **raise** babies and to sleep during the day.

They use their ears when they catch their **prey** at night.

When bats fly, they make some **sounds**.

Those sounds hit insects, and the echoes **bounce** back to the bats.

The bats fly fast and **grasp** the insects.

They help farmers by eating insects and saving crops.

Bats are a **symbol** of **death** in **Western** culture.

However, bats are a symbol of happiness in China.

● 해석 ●

박쥐의 일생

박쥐는 전 세계 거의 모든 곳에서 발견된다.

그러나 사람들은 그것들과 친밀하지 않다. 당신은 어떠한가?

박쥐를 좋아하는가?

그것들은 날 수 있는 유일한 포유동물이다.

그것들은 날개를 쭉 뻗어서 날갯짓을 할 수 있다.

많은 박쥐들은 나뭇가지에 매달려서 나무에 산다.

그것들 중 몇몇은 동굴 속에서 산다.

동굴은 새끼를 기르고 낮 동안에 자기에 완벽한 장소이다.

그것들은 밤에 먹이를 잡을 때 자신의 귀를 이용한다.

박쥐가 날 때, 그것들은 약간의 소리를 낸다.

그 소리는 곤충에 부딪치고, 메아리가 다시 박쥐에게로 되돌아온다.

박쥐는 빨리 날아 곤충들을 낚아챈다.

그것들은 곤충을 먹어서 곡식을 보호함으로써 농부를 돕는다.

서양 문화에서 박쥐는 죽음의 상징이다.

그러나 중국에서는 박쥐가 행복의 상징이다.

• Lesson 2 • **The Wonderful Flier of the Night** p.22

Ⓐ
1. dangle 2. shadow 3. ceiling
4. cave 5. flier 6. island
7. harm 8. calm 9. upside down
10. memorial

Ⓑ
1. village 2. mice 3. pocket 4. lonely

Ⓒ

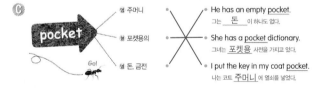

형 주머니
He has an empty **pocket**.
그는 ___돈___ 이 하나도 없다.

형 포켓용의
She has a **pocket** dictionary.
그녀는 포켓용 사전을 가지고 있다.

형 돈, 금전
I put the key in my coat **pocket**.
나는 코트 주머니 에 열쇠를 넣었다.

Ⓓ
1. island 2. village 3. memorial
4. lonely 5. shadow 6. cave
7. ceiling 8. dangled 9. upside down
10. calm 11. harm 12. pocket
13. flier 14. mouse

Ⓔ **The Wonderful Flier of the Night** p.25

Ted takes a trip to an **island**.

People say, "Don't go to the **cave**. A vampire bat will get you and **harm** you."

But he goes into the cave to study some insects.

He looks up at the **ceiling**.

Something is **dangling**.

It is **upside down** in the cave.

Both of them are very scared but stay **calm**.

It spreads its wings and makes a big **shadow**.

Ted says, "Oh, you're a **lonely** bat. I will be your friend."

He opens his **pocket**, and the vampire bat goes inside.

They go down to the **village**.

Big **mice** are bothering and biting people in the town.

The vampire bat flies up and traps them with its wings.

One day, the vampire bat disappeared.

To remember it, they built a **memorial** for the vampire bat: The Wonderful **Flier** of the Night.

● 해석 ●

밤의 멋진 비행사

테드는 섬으로 여행을 간다.

사람들은 말한다. "그 동굴에 가지 마라. 흡혈박쥐가 너를 잡아서 해칠 거야."

그러나 그는 곤충을 연구하기 위해서 동굴 안으로 들어간다.

그는 천장을 올려다본다.

무엇인가가 매달려 있다.

그것은 동굴 안에서 거꾸로 뒤집혀 있다.

테드와 그것 둘 다 매우 겁을 먹었지만 차분히 가만히 있다.

그것은 날개를 펼쳐 큰 그림자를 만든다.

테드는 말한다. "오, 너는 외로운 박쥐구나. 내가 네 친구가 되어줄게."

그가 그의 주머니를 열자, 흡혈박쥐는 안으로 들어간다.

그들은 마을로 내려간다.

큰 쥐들이 마을에서 사람들을 괴롭히고 물고 있다.

흡혈박쥐는 날아올라 날개로 쥐들을 잡는다.

어느 날, 흡혈박쥐는 사라졌다.

그것을 기억하기 위해, 사람들은 흡혈박쥐를 위한 기념비를 세웠다: 밤의 멋진 비행사.

Unit 3

Around the World
전 세계

• Lesson 1 • **New Year's Day** p.26

Ⓐ
1. past 2. calendar 3. delight 4. fancy
5. exchange 6. bamboo 7. countdown 8. envelope
9. festival 10. sweet

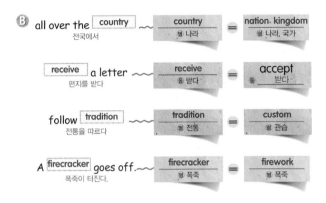

B all over the [country] ～ country 명 나라 = nation. kingdom 명 나라, 국가
전국에서

[receive] a letter ～ receive 통 받다 = accept 통 받다
편지를 받다

follow [tradition] ～ tradition 명 전통 = custom 명 관습
전통을 따르다

A [firecracker] goes off. ～ firecracker 명 폭죽 = firework 명 폭죽
폭죽이 터진다.

C 1. bamboo 2. fancy 3. sweets 4. envelope

D 1. calendar 2. past 3. received
4. delighted 5. exchanged, tradition
6. festival 7. country 8. firecrackers
9. countdown

E New Year's Day p.29

People happily wish others good luck on New Year's Day.
They look back on the **past** year and plan for the coming
new year. People all over the world celebrate the new
year in different ways. They celebrate the new year with
traditions from their **countries**.
Japanese people send and **receive** New Year's cards
and share warm wishes. They decorate their homes with
bamboo and pine branches.
In Mexico, people eat 12 grapes when the midnight
countdown begins. Each of the **sweet** grapes stands for
good luck for each month of the new year.
A **festival** is an important part of the New Year's
celebration in Brazil. People sing and dance while
dressed in **fancy** clothes.
Chinese people celebrate New Year's Day on the lunar
calendar. They put lucky money in red **envelopes**. Then,
they **exchange** them as gifts for the new year. They also
light **firecrackers** and enjoy lion dances in the street.
What New Year's Day celebration in your country **delights**
you?

● 해석 ●
설날
사람들은 설날에 행복하게 다른 사람들의 행운을 기원한다. 그들은 지난
해를 되돌아보고 다가오는 새해를 위한 계획을 세운다. 전 세계의 사람
들은 새해를 다른 방법으로 축하한다. 그들은 자기 나라의 전통에 따라
새해를 축하한다.
일본 사람들은 새해 카드를 보내고 받으며 훈훈한 소망을 나눈다. 그들

은 대나무와 소나무 가지로 자신들의 집을 장식한다.
멕시코에서, 사람들은 자정의 카운트다운이 시작될 때 12개의 포도 알을
먹는다. 각각의 달콤한 포도 알은 새해의 각 달의 행운을 나타낸다.
브라질에서 축제는 새해 축하의 중요한 부분이다. 사람들은 화려한 옷을
입고 노래를 부르며 춤을 춘다.
중국 사람들은 음력으로 새해를 축하한다. 그들은 행운의 돈을 빨간 봉
투들에 집어넣는다. 그 다음, 그들은 그것들을 새해의 선물로 교환한다.
그들은 또 거리에서 폭죽들을 쏘고 사자 춤을 즐긴다.
당신의 나라에서 당신을 즐겁게 하는 새해 축하에는 어떤 것이 있는가?

• Lesson 2 • **Losing a Tooth Customs** p.30

A 1. show up 2. couch 3. crow 4. wiggle
5. wrap 6. present 7. loose 8. be about to
9. pillow 10. fall asleep

B 1. Excuse 2. came out of 3. gold
4. put, in

C

present ～
형 출석한, 참석한
명 선물
형 현재, 지금
Go!

• I am satisfied with my life at present.
나는 현재 내 생활에 만족한다.
• He was present at the meeting.
그는 회의에 참석했다
• She got a birthday present.
그녀는 생일 선물 을 받았다.

D 1. present 2. gold 3. put, in, wrapped
4. showed up 5. came out of 6. Excuse
7. am about to 8. couch 9. pillow
10. crow 11. fall asleep 12. loose
13. wiggled

E Losing a Tooth Customs p.33

Tom invites some friends from different countries to his
house.
At lunch, Ted says to his friends, "My tooth is **loose**. It **is
about to** fall out."
He **wiggles** his tooth with his finger. Then, it **comes out of**
his mouth.
Marco from Spain says, "Oh, **put** your tooth **in** a mouse
hole. The Tooth Mouse will take it and give you a
present."
Nana from Greece says, "No, no. Throw it on the roof.
A **crow** will take it and give you a strong, new one."
Right after dinner, Ted puts his tooth under his **pillow**.
He lies on the **couch**. He **falls asleep** quickly.
Tara, the Tooth Fairy, **shows up** and tries to take his tooth.

Tara says, "**Excuse** me. Can I take your tooth?"

Ted wakes up and says sleepily, "No problem. I'll give it to you."

The Tooth Fairy **wraps** the tooth in paper.

The Tooth Fairy gives **gold** coins to Ted.

● 해석 ●

이를 빼는 관습

테드는 다른 나라에서 온 친구들 몇 명을 집에 초대한다.
점심 때, 테드는 친구들에게 말한다. "내 이가 흔들거려. 이게 막 빠지려고 해."
그는 손가락으로 자기 이를 흔든다. 그러자, 그것이 그의 입 밖으로 나온다.
스페인에서 온 마르코가 말한다. "오, 너의 이를 쥐구멍에 넣어. 이빨 쥐가 그것을 가져가고 너에게 선물을 줄 거야."
그리스에서 온 나나가 말한다. "아냐, 안돼. 그것을 지붕에 던져. 까마귀가 그것을 가져가고 너에게 튼튼한 새 이를 줄 거야."
저녁을 먹은 직후에, 테드는 그의 이를 베게 밑에 놓는다.
그는 소파에 눕는다. 그는 빠르게 잠이 든다.
이의 요정 타라가 나타나 그의 이를 가져가려고 한다.
타라는 말한다. "실례합니다. 당신의 이를 가져가도 될까요?"
테드는 깨서 나른하게 말한다. "물론이죠. 당신에게 그것을 드릴게요."
이의 요정은 이를 종이에 싼다.
이의 요정은 테드에게 금화를 준다.

Unit 4

Life Cycle
생활 주기

● Lesson 1 ● **The Life Cycle of a Frog** p.34

Ⓐ 1. tadpole 2. hatch 3. froglet
4. lung 5. life cycle 6. be covered with
7. again 8. amphibian 9. gills
10. germinate

Ⓑ
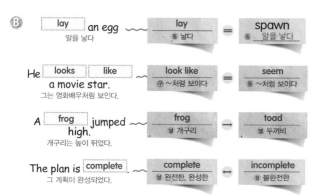

Ⓒ 1. germinate 2. is covered with 3. tadpole
4. hatch

Ⓓ 1. complete 2. amphibians 3. frog
4. looks like 5. life cycle 6. again
7. lays 8. gills 9. froglets
10. lungs

Ⓔ **The Life Cycle of a Frog** p.37

In spring, seeds **germinate** and flowers bloom.

"Ribbit! Ribbit" A **frog** is in the pond.

A frog is an **amphibian**. A frog **lays** many eggs in the water.

Frog eggs **are covered with** a jellylike coating.

About 6 to 21 days later, the eggs **hatch**.

7 to 10 days later, a **tadpole** begins to swim.

After about 6 to 9 weeks, little legs start to sprout.

A tadpole breathes with its **gills** in the water.

As it grows, the gills disappear, and **lungs** form.

After about 9 weeks, a tadpole **looks like** a young frog with a tail. We call it a **froglet**.

By 12 to 16 weeks, a frog's growth is **complete**.

The frog lays eggs in the water, and the cycle begins **again**.

The **life cycle** of a frog continues.

● 해석 ●

개구리의 생활 주기

봄에는 씨앗이 싹트고 꽃이 핀다.
"개굴! 개굴!" 개구리가 연못에 있다.
개구리는 양서류이다. 개구리는 물속에 많은 알을 낳는다.
개구리 알은 젤리 같은 막으로 덮여 있다.
약 6일에서 21일 후에, 알은 부화한다.
7일에서 10일 후에, 올챙이가 헤엄을 치기 시작한다.
약 6주에서 9주 후에, 작은 다리들이 자라나기 시작한다.
올챙이는 물속에서 아가미로 호흡한다.
자라면서, 아가미는 사라지고 허파가 만들어진다.
약 9주 후에, 올챙이는 꼬리를 가진 어린 개구리처럼 보인다. 우리는 그것을 새끼 개구리라고 부른다.
12주에서 16주까지, 개구리의 성장은 완성된다.
개구리는 물속에다 알을 낳고, 순환은 다시 시작된다.
개구리의 생활 주기는 계속된다.

• Lesson 2 • **Turn Back Time**   p.38

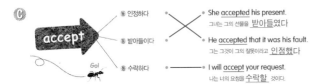

A
1. ugly
2. apologize
3. look down on
4. new
5. accept
6. turn back
7. age
8. avoid
9. why
10. recognize

B
1. Whenever, unbelievable
2. explain
3. behave

C

accept
- 통 인정하다 —— He accepted that it was his fault.
  그는 그것이 그의 잘못이라고 <u>인정했</u>다
- 통 받아들이다 —— She accepted his present.
  그녀는 그의 선물을 <u>받아들였</u>다
- 통 수락하다 —— I will accept your request.
  나는 너의 요청을 <u>수락할</u> 것이다.

D
1. new
2. ugly
3. age
4. recognize
5. why
6. explain
7. behaves
8. looks down on
9. avoid
10. apologizes
11. accept
12. Whenever
13. unbelievable
14. turn back

E **Turn Back Time**   p.41

Ted **behaved** very rudely to his parents and friends when he was 7.

One day, something **unbelievable** happened to him.

When he looked in the mirror, he looked older than the other boys his **age**.

"Oh, no! I'm so **ugly**! I look like an old man."

Ted was sad, so he **avoided** going outside. Ted regretted his bad behavior.

Whenever he behaved well, he became younger.

Good behavior **turned back** time.

"Ted, **why** don't you go outside and play with your friends?" Mom asked.

Ted went outside. His friends didn't **recognize** him.

"Who are you? Are you **new**?"

"No, I'm not new. I'm Ted." Ted **explained** what had happened to him.

They were surprised and felt sorry for him.

Ted **apologized** to his friends.

"I'm sorry for hurting you. I **looked down on** you before."

Ted's friends **accepted** his apology and played with him.

Ted thought, "I will be a better person from now on."

● 해석 ●

시간을 되돌리다

7세 때, 테드는 부모님과 친구들에게 매우 무례하게 행동했다.

어느 날, 믿을 수 없는 어떤 일이 그에게 일어났다.

그가 거울을 보았을 때, 그는 그 나이 또래의 다른 소년들보다 더 나이 들어 보였다.

"오, 안돼! 나는 너무 못생겼어! 나는 노인처럼 보여."

테드는 슬퍼서 밖에 나가는 것을 피했다. 테드는 그의 나쁜 행동을 후회했다.

그가 착하게 행동할 때마다, 그는 더 어려졌다.

착한 행동은 시간을 되돌렸다.

"테드야, 밖에 나가서 네 친구들과 노는 것이 어떠니?" 엄마가 말했다.

테드는 밖으로 나갔다. 그의 친구들은 그를 알아보지 못했다.

"너는 누구니? 새로 온 아이니?"

"아니, 난 새로 온 아이가 아니야. 나는 테드야." 테드는 그에게 어떤 일이 일어났었는지 설명했다.

친구들은 놀랐고 그의 일을 유감스러워했다.

테드는 친구들에게 사과했다.

"너희들 마음을 아프게 해서 미안해. 전에 나는 너희들을 업신여겼어."

테드의 친구들은 그의 사과를 받아들이고 그와 함께 놀았다.

테드는 생각했다. '나는 이제부터 더 나은 사람이 될 거야.'

Unit 5
Space
우주

• Lesson 1 • **From the Earth to the Moon**   p.42

A
1. footprint
2. alarm
3. spacecraft
4. deal
5. data
6. astronaut
7. launch
8. moon
9. fine
10. circle

B
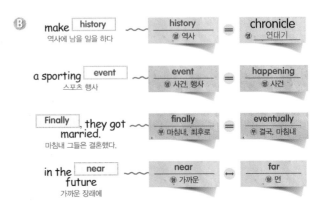

make history — history 명 역사 = chronicle 명 연대기
역사에 남을 일을 하다

a sporting event — event 명 사건, 행사 = happening 명 사건
스포츠 행사

Finally, they got married. — finally 부 마침내, 최후로 = eventually 부 결국, 마침내
마침내 그들은 결혼했다.

in the near future — near 형 가까운 ⟷ far 형 먼
가까운 장래에

Ⓒ 1. circles 2. astronaut 3. alarm 4. footprints

Ⓓ 1. near 2. spacecraft 3. launched 4. event
5. moon 6. data 7. fine 8. dealt
9. Finally 10. history

Ⓔ **From the Earth to the Moon** p.45

Apollo 11 was an American **spacecraft**.

Three **astronauts** were aboard *Apollo 11* in July 1969.

They were on a mission to explore the **moon**.

Many people gathered **near** the space center.

Millions watched the **event** on television.

A rocket carrying *Apollo 11* was **launched**.

Apollo 11 **circled** the Earth and then flew to the moon.

The **alarm** went off while landing on the moon.

There was trouble with the computer **data**.

But the astronauts **dealt** with the problem calmly.

They **finally** landed on the moon.

The astronauts stepped off *Apollo 11*.

The surface was covered with a **fine** powder.

They left the first **footprints** on the moon.

The **history** of space travel to the moon began with *Apollo 11*.

● 해석 ●
지구에서 달까지
아폴로 11호는 미국의 우주선이었다.
세 명의 우주비행사가 1969년 7월에 아폴로 11호에 탑승했다.
그들에게는 달을 탐사하는 임무가 있었다.
많은 사람들이 우주 센터 가까이에 모였다.
수백만 명의 사람들이 TV로 그 사건을 보았다.
아폴로 11호를 탑재한 로켓이 발사되었다.
아폴로 11호는 지구를 회전한 다음 달로 날아갔다.
달에 착륙하는 동안 경보가 울렸다.
컴퓨터 데이터에 문제가 있었다.
그러나 우주비행사들이 침착하게 그 문제를 해결했다.
그들은 마침내 달에 착륙했다.
우주비행사들은 아폴로 11호에서 내렸다.
그 표면은 미세한 먼지로 뒤덮여 있었다.
그들은 달에 첫 발자국들을 남겼다.
달로 가는 우주 여행의 역사는 아폴로 11호와 함께 시작되었다.

• Lesson 2 • **Fly Me to Mars** p.46

Ⓐ 1. discuss 2. beg 3. plate 4. holiday
5. space 6. Mars 7. alien 8. suggest
9. spacesuit 10. weird

Ⓑ 1. hill 2. equipment 3. telescope 4. satellite

Ⓒ

Ⓓ 1. holiday 2. hill 3. plates 4. begged
5. discussed 6. space 7. equipment 8. telescope
9. spacesuits 10. satellite 11. Mars 12. weird
13. aliens 14. suggested

Ⓔ **Fly Me to Mars** p.49

Ted is really into stories about **space**.

He hopes to meet **aliens**.

But everybody laughs at his **weird** ideas.

One day, a girl named Tara came to Ted.

She **suggests** spending the summer **holiday** in space.

They **discuss** their plans for the space trip.

"We need **spacesuits**, food, and a camera."

They get all the **equipment** ready for the trip.

"We're ready! Let's go." They go up the **hill**.

They look up at the sky through a **telescope**.

A shooting star falls, and Tara says, "Now!"

Ted turns on the **satellite** radio.

Somebody talks to them. "I'm Sevi from **Mars**."

Ted and Tara **beg** her, "Can you fly us to Mars?"

The UFO is like a flying **plate**. It lands on the hill.

Ted and Tara get in the UFO and wave goodbye to the Earth.

● 해석 ●
화성으로 나를 데려다 줘
테드는 우주에 관한 이야기에 흠뻑 빠져 있다.
그는 외계인을 만나고 싶다.
그러나 모두 그의 이상한 생각을 비웃는다.
어느 날, 타라라는 여자 아이가 테드에게 왔다.
그녀는 우주에서 여름 방학을 보내자고 제안한다.
그들은 우주 여행에 대한 계획들을 논의한다.
"우리는 우주복, 음식, 그리고 카메라가 필요해."
그들은 여행에 필요한 모든 장비를 준비한다.
"우리는 준비됐어! 가자." 그들은 언덕으로 올라간다.
그들은 망원경으로 하늘을 올려다본다.
유성이 떨어지고, 타라가 말한다. "지금이야!"
테드가 인공위성 라디오를 켠다.
누군가 그들에게 말한다. "나는 화성에서 온 세비야."
테드와 타라는 그녀에게 애원한다. "우리를 화성으로 데려다 줄 수 있어?"
UFO는 나는 접시처럼 생겼다. 그것은 언덕에 착륙한다.
테드와 타라는 UFO에 올라타고 지구를 향해 작별인사를 한다.

Unit 6

The Ocean
해양

• Lesson 1 • **The Life of a Salmon** p.50

Ⓐ 1. female   2. instinct   3. salt   4. return
5. survive   6. salmon   7. rock   8. enter
9. stream   10. migration

Ⓑ

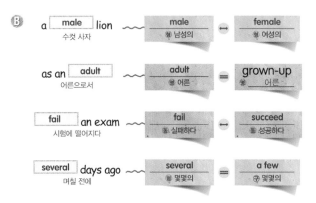

a ⌐male⌐ lion   male ⑱ 남성의 ⟷ female ⑱ 여성의
   수컷 사자

as an ⌐adult⌐   adult ⑱ 어른 = grown-up ⑱ 어른
   어른으로서

⌐fail⌐ an exam   fail ⑤ 실패하다 ⟷ succeed ⑤ 성공하다
   시험에 떨어지다

⌐several⌐ days ago   several ⑱ 몇몇의 = a few ⓐ 몇몇의
   며칠 전에

Ⓒ 1. salt   2. enter   3. Several   4. salmon

Ⓓ 1. stream   2. rocks   3. failed   4. male
5. female   6. instinct   7. migration   8. adult
9. returns   10. survive

Ⓔ The Life of a Salmon p.53

Here is a cold and clear **stream**.
Some tiny baby **salmon** swim in the fresh water.
They start their **migration** to the ocean.
Their bodies change to live in **salt** water.
At last, they **enter** the ocean.
They grow into **adult** salmon in the ocean.
Some of them **fail** to live in the big ocean.
Only a few of them **survive** among the saltwater fish.
They leave the ocean after **several** years.
They try to **return** to their stream.
They have the **instinct** to go back home.
After arriving, the salmon lay eggs among the **rocks**.
Female salmon lay thousands of eggs. **Male** salmon help them.

Soon after, both the female and male salmon die.
The life of a salmon begins and ends in the same place.

● 해석 ●
연어의 삶
여기 차갑고 맑은 개울이 있다.
아주 작은 아기 연어들 몇몇이 민물에서 수영한다.
그들은 바다로 이주를 시작한다.
그들의 몸은 바닷물에서 살 수 있게끔 변한다.
마침내, 그들은 바다에 들어간다.
그들은 바다에서 어른 연어들로 자란다.
그들 중 일부는 큰 바다에서 사는 데 실패한다.
그들 중 단지 몇몇만 바닷물고기 사이에서 살아남는다.
그들은 여러 해 후에 바다를 떠난다.
그들은 그들의 개울로 다시 돌아가기 위해 노력한다.
그들은 고향으로 돌아가려는 본능이 있다.
도착한 후에, 연어들은 바위 사이에 알을 낳는다.
암컷 연어들은 수천 개의 알을 낳는다. 수컷 연어들은 그들을 돕는다.
그리고 얼마 안 있어 암컷과 수컷 연어는 죽는다.
연어의 삶은 같은 장소에서 시작하고 끝난다.

• Lesson 2 • **Pirates and Treasure** p.54

Ⓐ 1. ship   2. take over   3. pirate   4. treasure
5. cruise   6. sweep   7. passenger   8. captain
9. terrible   10. often

Ⓑ 1. area   2. threatened   3. search   4. away

Ⓒ

search
⑤ 검색하다
⑤ 수색하다
Go!
⑤ 찾다

He is searching for missing people in an accident.
그는 사고로 실종된 사람들을 찾고 있다

I searched for information on the Internet. 나는 인터넷에서 정보를 검색했다

The police searched the house.
경찰이 집을 수색했다

Ⓓ 1. terrible   2. area   3. pirates
4. often, ships   5. took over   6. threatened
7. cruise   8. swept   9. passengers
10. captain   11. search   12. treasure
13. away

Ⓔ Pirates and Treasure p.57

Ted takes a **cruise** with his family.
Ted is very excited to sail the south ocean.
Ted asks the **captain**, "Will we have a chance to see any **pirates**?"
He answers, "Well, the west side is the dangerous **area**.

Pirates **often** sail there. But we never go that far."

Ted has fun on the **ship** in the calm ocean.

That night, a **terrible** storm blows.

The ship is **swept** to the west side of the ocean.

At last, the storm destroys the ship.

In the morning, scary pirates **take over** the ship.

Then they **threaten** the **passengers**.

Ted decides to save everyone and shouts at the pirates,

"There is a prince among the passengers. He has a big
treasure chest under his bed. You can take it!"

The pirates **search** for the treasure chest.

Ted and the other passengers take the pirates' ship and
sail **away**.

● 해석 ●

해적과 보물

테드는 가족들과 함께 유람선 여행을 한다.

테드는 남쪽 바다를 항해하는 것에 매우 신나있다.

테드가 선장에게 묻는다. "우리가 해적을 볼 기회가 있을까요?"

그가 대답한다. "글쎄요, 서쪽은 위험한 지역이죠. 해적들이 종종 그곳을
항해해요. 하지만 우리는 그렇게까지 멀리는 절대 안 가요."

테드는 고요한 바다에 있는 배에서 즐거움을 만끽한다.

그날 밤, 지독한 폭풍이 몰아친다.

배가 바다의 서쪽으로 쓸려간다.

결국, 폭풍은 배를 파괴한다.

아침에 무서운 해적들이 배를 차지한다.

그러고 나서 그들은 승객들을 협박한다.

테드는 모두를 구하기로 마음먹고 해적들에게 소리친다.

"승객들 중에 왕자가 있어요. 그는 침대 밑에 커다란 보물상자를 가지고
있죠. 당신들이 가져가세요!"

해적들은 보물상자를 찾아 다닌다.

테드와 다른 승객들은 해적들의 배를 타고 달아난다.

Unit 7
Great Adventures
위대한 모험들

• Lesson 1 • **The Second to Reach the South Pole**   p.58

Ⓐ 1. exhausted   2. shore   3. the English   4. polar
   5. national   6. suffer   7. frostbite   8. prepare
   9. vehicle   10. expedition

Ⓑ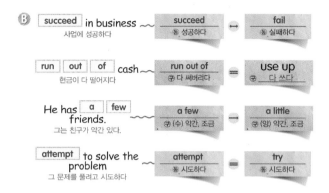

Ⓒ 1. vehicle   2. a few   3. expedition   4. exhausted

Ⓓ 1. succeeded 2. shore   3. attempted   4. run out of
   5. the English 6. suffered   7. prepared   8. frostbite
   9. polar   10. national

Ⓔ **The Second to Reach the South Pole**   p.61

The **polar** adventure began in the nineteenth century.

Many **expeditions** had tried to reach the South Pole
before 1912.

But nobody **succeeded** at getting to the South Pole.

Robert Scott was the leader of the English expedition.

His expedition **attempted** to be the first to get to the
South Pole.

They set up a base camp on the **shore**.

They carefully **prepared** the expedition.

They took sled dogs, ponies, and **vehicles**.

When they arrived at the South Pole, the Norwegian flag
was flying.

The Norwegians reached the South Pole 5 weeks before
the English.

They were very disappointed and **exhausted**.

They **suffered** from the bad weather on their way back.

They became ill and got **frostbite**.

They **ran out of** food and died of hunger.

They were found **a few** kilometers from their base camp.

They failed but became **national** heroes.

● 해석 ●

남극에 두 번째로 도착한 사람들

극지의 모험은 19세기에 시작되었다.

1912년 이전에 많은 탐험대들이 남극에 도달하고자 애썼다.

하지만 어느 누구도 남극에 도달하는 데 성공하지 못했다.

로버트 스캇은 영국 탐험대의 대장이었다.

그의 탐험대는 남극에 처음으로 도착하고자 시도했다.

그들은 해안가에 베이스 캠프를 차렸다.

그들은 신중하게 탐험을 준비했다.

그들은 개 썰매, 조랑말과 탈것들을 가지고 갔다.
그들이 남극에 도착했을 때, 노르웨이 깃발이 휘날리고 있었다.
노르웨이 사람들이 영국 사람들보다 5주 전에 먼저 남극에 도착했던 것이다.
그들은 매우 실망했고 기진맥진했다.
그들은 돌아오는 길에 악천후로 고생했다.
그들은 아팠고, 동상에 걸렸다.
그들은 음식이 다 떨어져서 굶어 죽었다.
그들은 그들의 베이스 캠프로부터 몇 킬로미터 떨어진 곳에서 발견되었다.
그들은 실패했지만 국가의 영웅들이 되었다.

• Lesson 2 • **The Mystery of the Devil's Triangle** p.62

Ⓐ 1. draw into 2. triangle 3. press 4. hero
5. whirlpool 6. submarine 7. bubble 8. reason
9. screen 10. theater

Ⓑ 1. daughter 2. situation 3. getting worse
4. bacteria

Ⓒ

Ⓓ 1. theater 2. screen 3. *Whirlpool* 4. Triangle
5. hero 6. submarine 7. drawn into 8. pressed
9. got worse 10. situation 11. daughter
12. bubbles 13. reason 14. Bacteria

Ⓔ **The Mystery of the Devil's Triangle** p.65

Ted watched a movie at the **theater**.
It was an adventure film about the Devil's **Triangle**.
A scientist lost her **daughter** in the Devil's Triangle.
Many ships and airplanes mysteriously disappeared there.
Ted says, "I want to discover the **reason** they went missing."
At that moment, Ted falls into the **screen**.
Ted and a scientist get in a **submarine** and go on an expedition.
Suddenly, a **whirlpool** forms near the Devil's Triangle.
The submarine is **drawn into** the hole.
Gas **bubbles** up from the bottom of the sea.

Ted shouts, "It is **getting worse**. The **situation** is very bad. We are sinking because of the gas bubbles."
The scientist **presses** a button.
Then, a lot of **bacteria** come out and catch the gas bubbles.
They solve the mystery of the Devil's Triangle and become **heroes**.

● 해석
악마의 삼각형에 관한 수수께끼
테드는 극장에서 영화를 보았다.
마의 삼각 지대에 관한 모험영화였다.
한 과학자가 마의 삼각 지대 안에서 그녀의 딸을 잃어버렸다.
많은 배와 비행기들이 이상하게도 그곳에서 사라졌다.
테드는 "나는 그들이 사라진 이유를 밝혀내고 싶어."라고 말한다.
그때, 테드는 화면 속으로 들어간다.
테드와 한 과학자가 잠수함을 타고 모험을 떠난다.
갑자기, 마의 삼각 지대 근처에서 소용돌이가 생겨난다.
잠수함이 구멍 안으로 끌려들어 간다.
바다 바닥으로부터 공기 거품이 올라온다.
테드가 소리친다. "점점 심해져요. 상황이 매우 나빠요. 공기 거품 때문에 우리가 가라앉고 있어요."
과학자가 버튼을 누른다.
그러자 많은 세균들이 나와서 공기 거품들을 잡는다.
그들은 마의 삼각 지대의 수수께끼를 풀고 영웅들이 된다.

Unit 8
The Honor
명예

• Lesson 1 • **The Nobel Prize** p.66

Ⓐ 1. anniversary 2. ceremony 3. establish
4. physics 5. be noted for 6. cash
7. since 8. literature 9. consist
10. corner

Ⓑ

C 1. corner   2. literature   3. cash   4. ceremony

D 1. international   2. honor   3. Since, physics
4. consists   5. wealth   6. is noted for
7. established   8. more than   9. anniversary

E ## The Nobel Prize   p.69

The Nobel Prize is an **international** award.
It awards people from all **corners** of the world.
It **honors** the people who did the best work in six different fields each year.
Three fields are in science. They are **physics**, chemistry, and medicine.
The others are **literature**, economic sciences, and work for world peace.
Alfred Nobel **established** the prize.
He was an inventor and businessman.
He **is noted for** his invention of dynamite.
He left much of his **wealth** to establish the Nobel Prize.
The Nobel Prize has been awarded **since** 1901.
Every prize **consists** of a diploma and a medal.
There are also **cash** awards.
The awards **ceremonies** are held in Sweden and Norway.
They are on December 10, the **anniversary** of Nobel's death.
More than 800 people have received prizes so far.
Who do you think the next Nobel Prize winner will be?

● 해석 ●
노벨상
노벨상은 국제적인 상이다.
이것은 세계 각지의 사람들에게 수여한다.
이것은 매년 여섯 개의 다른 분야에서 최고의 업적을 이룬 사람들에게 명예를 준다.
세 개의 분야는 과학 분야이다. 그것은 물리학, 화학, 약학이다.
다른 분야들은 문학과 경제학, 세계평화이다.
알프레드 노벨이 이 상을 설립했다.
그는 발명가이자 사업가였다.
그는 그의 발명품인 다이너마이트로 유명하다.
그는 노벨상을 설립하기 위해 자신의 많은 재산을 남겼다.
노벨상은 1901년 이래로 계속 수여되고 있다.
모든 상은 증서와 메달로 구성되어 있다.
또한 상금도 있다.
상 수식은 스웨덴과 노르웨이에서 열린다.
노벨의 기일인 12월 10일이다.
지금까지 800명 이상의 사람들이 상을 받았다.
당신은 다음 노벨상 수상자가 누구일 거라고 생각하는가?

• Lesson 2 • **The Funny Winner**   p.70

A 1. question   2. break wind   3. correct   4. know
5. dictionary   6. bloat   7. participate   8. chance
9. advance   10. everybody

B 1. competition   2. confident   3. mistake
4. giggled

C
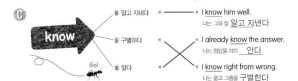

D 1. bloated   2. competition   3. advanced
4. participated   5. Everybody   6. chance
7. mistake   8. break wind   9. giggled
10. question   11. know   12. correct
13. dictionary   14. confident

E ## The Funny Winner   p.73

Ted **knows** many words and likes to find the meanings of difficult words.
Every day, he reads many books and the **dictionary**.
One day, he **participates** in a spelling bee.
Ted and a girl **advance** to the final round.
The girl looks very smart and **confident**.
She says, "I will be the winner of this **competition**."
Almost **everybody** expects her to win.
But she gets confused and makes a **mistake**.
The host says, "Now it's your **chance**, Ted."
He asks the final **question** to Ted.
Ted feels **bloated** and can't answer.
"Well, the answer is … The answer is …"
Suddenly, he **breaks wind** very loudly.
People start to **giggle**, so Ted feels nervous.
"Ha-ha-ha. The answer is b-l-i-z-z-a-r-d."
"Wow, that's **correct**! You are the funny winner of the spelling bee."

● 해석 ●
웃기는 우승자
테드는 많은 단어를 알고 있고, 어려운 단어들의 뜻을 알아내는 것을 좋아한다.
매일, 그는 많은 책들과 사전을 읽는다.
어느 날, 그는 철자법 대회에 참가한다.

테드와 한 소녀가 결승에 진출한다.
그 소녀는 매우 총명하고 자신감이 넘쳐 보인다.
"내가 이 대회의 우승자가 될 거야."라고 그녀는 말한다.
거의 모든 사람들이 그녀가 우승할 것이라고 기대한다.
그러나 그녀는 헷갈려서 실수를 한다.
대회 진행자가 말한다. "이제 당신의 기회입니다, 테드."
그는 마지막 질문을 테드에게 한다.
테드는 배가 터질 것 같아서 대답을 할 수 없다.
"음, 정답은 … 정답은 …"
갑자기, 그는 아주 크게 방귀를 뀐다.
사람들이 낄낄 웃기 시작해서 테드는 긴장한다.
"하, 하, 하. 정답은 b-l-i-z-z-a-r-d입니다."
"와우, 정답입니다! 당신이 이번 철자법 대회의 웃기는 우승자네요."

Unit 9 — Step Back in Time
과거로 되돌아 가다

• Lesson 1 • **The Lost City of Pompeii** p.74

Ⓐ 1. disaster   2. remain   3. archaeologist
   4. mountain   5. bath   6. shop
   7. bury   8. ash   9. petrify
   10. volcano

Ⓑ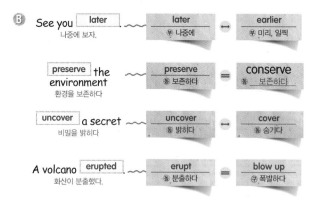

See you [later] — later 및 나중에 ⟷ earlier 및 미리, 일찍
나중에 보자.

[preserve] the environment — preserve 통 보존하다 = conserve 통 보존하다
환경을 보존하다

[uncover] a secret — uncover 통 밝히다 ⟷ cover 통 숨기다
비밀을 밝히다

A volcano [erupted] — erupt 통 분출하다 = blow up 주 폭발하다
화산이 분출했다.

Ⓒ 1. shop   2. bath   3. mountain   4. buried

Ⓓ 1. archaeologist   2. ash   3. remained
   4. mountain, volcano   5. erupted
   6. Later   7. petrified   8. preserved
   9. disaster   10. uncovered

Ⓔ **The Lost City of Pompeii** p.77

Pompeii was an ancient Roman city.
It had a large market, a theater, and many <u>shops</u>.
Many people enjoyed taking <u>baths</u> and relaxing in Pompeii.
A <u>mountain</u> and the sea were near the city.
One day, the mountain <u>erupted</u>. In other words, a <u>volcano</u> erupted.
Gas, <u>ash</u>, and rocks covered the city.
The people of the ancient city of Pompeii did not have a chance to escape.
Pompeii was quickly <u>buried</u> by the volcanic eruption.
The <u>disaster</u> of Pompeii was forgotten.
1,700 years <u>later</u>, people found the lost city of Pompeii.
They <u>uncovered</u> some Roman paintings.
<u>Archaeologists</u> came and dug up the remains of the city.
A lot of <u>petrified</u> bodies of people and animals were discovered.
They were <u>preserved</u> well by the ash and mud.
Surprisingly, some buildings, houses, and streets <u>remained</u>.
Now we can visit Pompeii and learn about life in ancient Rome.

● 해석 ●
잃어버린 도시 폼페이
폼페이는 고대 로마의 도시였다.
그곳에는 큰 시장과 극장, 그리고 많은 가게들이 있었다.
많은 사람들은 폼페이에서 목욕을 하고 휴식을 취하기를 즐겼다.
도시 근처에는 산과 바다가 있었다.
어느 날, 그 산이 폭발했다. 다시 말해서, 화산이 분출한 것이다.
가스, 화산재, 그리고 바위들이 그 도시를 뒤덮었다.
고대 도시 폼페이 사람들은 도망갈 기회가 없었다.
폼페이는 화산 분출에 의해 빠르게 파묻혔다.
폼페이의 재난은 잊혀졌다.
1700년이 지나, 사람들은 잃어버린 도시 폼페이를 찾아냈다.
그들은 로마의 그림 몇 점을 발견했다.
고고학자들이 와서 도시의 유적들을 파헤쳤다.
사람과 동물의 석화된 사체들이 많이 발견되었다.
그것들은 화산재와 진흙에 의해 잘 보존되었다.
놀랍게도, 몇몇 건축물과 집, 그리고 거리들이 남아 있었다.
이제 우리는 폼페이를 방문해서 고대 로마의 삶에 대해 배울 수 있다.

• Lesson 2 • **The Stone Age** p.78

Ⓐ 1. create   2. point   3. set   4. spin
   5. wonder   6. faint   7. tool   8. clock

9. raw 10. surround

B 1. Stone Age 2. knives 3. sharp 4. edges

C

봉 놓다

봉 조정하다, 맞추다

명 한 벌, 한 세트

I bought a chess set.
나는 체스 한 세트를 샀다.

He set a cup on the table.
그는 컵을 탁자 위에 놓았다.

She set a dial on the oven.
그녀는 오븐의 다이얼을 조정했다.

D 1. clock 2. pointing 3. Stone Age 4. tool
5. Knives 6. sharp 7. edges 8. set
9. surrounded 10. faint 11. spun 12. raw
13. wonder 14. created

E **The Stone Age** p.81

Ted looks at the **clock** in the morning.

It stops and **points** at 12.

He tries to **set** the clock.

But it suddenly **spins** back.

Ted feels dizzy and **faints**.

When he wakes up, he is **surrounded** by people.

A woman smiles, "Don't worry. We will take care of you."

They look like people from the **Stone Age** because they
are wearing animal skins.

The men go hunting with stone **tools**.

But the stone tools are not **sharp**.

Ted breaks and sharpens the **edge** of a stone.

It becomes a sharp stone **knife**.

People look at Ted and **wonder** where he came from.

People hunt a bear and cut meat with stone knives.

Ted says, "Wait! Don't eat **raw** meat."

Ted rubs two stones together and makes a fire.

People shout, "You **created** fire! You're our king!"

● 해석 ●

석기 시대

테드는 아침에 시계를 본다.

그것은 멈추어서 숫자 12를 가리킨다.

그는 시계를 맞추려고 한다.

하지만 그것이 갑자기 거꾸로 돈다.

테드는 어지러움을 느끼며 기절한다.

그가 깨어났을 때, 그는 사람들에게 둘러싸여 있다.

한 여자가 웃는다. "걱정하지 말아요. 우리가 당신을 보호해 줄 거예요."

그들은 동물 가죽을 입고 있기 때문에 석기 시대에서 온 사람들 같아 보인다.

남자들은 돌로 된 도구들을 갖고 사냥하러 간다.

그러나 돌로 된 도구들은 날카롭지 않다.

테드는 돌의 가장자리를 부숴 날카롭게 한다.

그것은 날카로운 돌칼이 된다.

사람들은 테드를 보며 그가 어디에서 왔는지 궁금해한다.

사람들은 곰을 사냥해서 돌칼로 고기를 자른다.

테드는 말한다. "기다려요! 날고기를 먹지 말아요."

테드는 두 개의 돌을 서로 문질러서 불을 만든다.

사람들은 소리친다. "당신이 불을 만들었어요! 당신은 우리의 왕이에요!"

Unit 10

World Landmark

세계의 랜드마크

● Lesson 1 ● **The Leaning Tower of Pisa** p.82

A 1. even though 2. effort 3. remarkable
4. bell 5. construction 6. belong
7. degree 8. cease 9. marble
10. foundation

B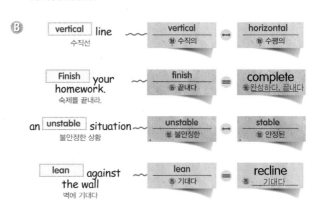

vertical line
수직선

vertical
형 수직의

⟷ horizontal
형 수평의

Finish your
homework.
숙제를 끝내라.

finish
끝내다

= complete
통 완성하다, 끝내다

an unstable situation
불안정한 상황

unstable
형 불안정한

⟷ stable
형 안정된

lean against
the wall
벽에 기대다

lean
통 기대다

= recline
통 기대다

C 1. construction 2. Even though 3. marble 4. lean

D 1. degree 2. belong 3. remarkable 4. vertical
5. bell 6. finished 7. foundation 8. ceased
9. effort 10. unstable

E **The Leaning Tower of Pisa** p.85

The Leaning Tower of Pisa is a famous **bell** tower in the
Italian city of Pisa.

The tower **belongs** to the church of Pisa.

It has 8 stories covered in white **marble**.

They began building the tower in 1173.

It was originally designed to be **vertical**.

But it began to sink after **construction** on the third floor in
1178.

Why did the tower sink and **lean**?

The tower was built on weak, **unstable** ground.

The builders made an **effort** to stop it from sinking.

After several attempts, they **ceased** building the tower for a century.

When the **foundation** became more stable, it was built again.

They **finished** building the tower and added five more floors 200 years later.

It leans at an angle of about 3.99 **degrees** now and continues to sink slowly.

Even though it leans, it looks attractive.

Many tourists visit this **remarkable** tower and take pictures.

● 해석 ●

피사의 사탑

피사의 사탑은 이탈리아의 도시 피사에 있는 유명한 종탑이다.

그 탑은 피사의 교회에 소속되어 있다.

그것은 흰 대리석으로 덮여 있는 8층짜리이다.

사람들은 1173년에 그 탑을 짓기 시작했다.

그것은 원래 수직으로 디자인되었다.

그러나 1178년에 3층을 건설한 이후에 내려앉기 시작했다.

왜 그 탑이 내려앉고 기울어졌을까?

탑은 약하고 불안정한 땅 위에 지어졌다.

건축가들은 탑이 내려앉는 것을 멈추기 위해 노력했다.

몇 번의 시도 후에, 그들은 100년 동안 탑 짓는 것을 중단했다.

기반이 더 안정되었을 때, 탑은 다시 지어졌다.

그들은 탑 짓기를 끝마쳤고 200년 후에 다섯 층을 더 지었다.

그것은 현재 약 3.99도 각도로 기울어 있으며 계속 천천히 내려앉고 있다.

비록 기울어져 있지만, 그 탑은 매력적으로 보인다.

많은 관광객들이 이 놀라운 탑을 방문해서 사진을 찍는다.

• Lesson 2 • **Climbing a Bridge** p.86

Ⓐ 1. beside　　　　2. neighbor　　　3. early

4. shock　　　　5. steep　　　　6. guardrail

7. mind one's step　8. on air　　　9. rope

10. tight

Ⓑ 1. Bridge　　　　2. landmark　　　3. walked across

4. missed my step

Ⓒ

tight

월 단단한　　　　　I'm going through a **tight** situation.
　　　　　　　　나는 <u>곤란한</u> 상황을 겪고 있는 중이다.

월 꽉 조이는　　　This shirt is too **tight** for me.
　　　　　　　　이 셔츠는 나에게 너무 <u>꽉 조인다</u>

월 곤란한　　　　I made a **tight** knot.
Go!　　　　　　나는 <u>단단한</u> 매듭을 지었다.

Ⓓ 1. steep　　　　2. beside　　　　3. landmark

4. on air　　　　5. Early　　　　6. rope

7. tight　　　　8. neighbor　　　9. bridge

10. Mind your step　11. walked across　12. missed my step

13. shocked　　　　14. guardrail

Ⓔ **Climbing a Bridge** p.89

Ted leaves home **early** in the morning.

He goes on a picnic with his **neighbor** Sam.

Sam is good at climbing **steep** walls.

So people call him "Spider Sam."

They arrive at a wide river **beside** a park.

There's a **bridge** over the river.

It is narrow and made of **rope**.

They **walk across** the bridge to get to the park.

When they reach the middle of the bridge, Sam **misses his step**.

Ted is **shocked** and shouts, "Watch out! **Mind your step**!"

Sam hangs and dangles from the rope.

Ted shouts, "Hold on **tight**."

Sam moves up the **guardrail** and climbs back onto the bridge.

"Oh, this bridge is perfect for climbing on."

His brave act on the bridge is put **on air**.

After that, the bridge becomes a famous **landmark** around the world.

● 해석 ●

다리 오르기

테드는 아침 일찍 집을 떠난다.

그는 그의 이웃인 샘과 소풍을 간다.

샘은 가파른 벽을 잘 탄다.

그래서 사람들은 그를 '거미 샘'이라고 부른다.

그들은 공원 옆의 넓은 강에 도착한다.

강 위에는 다리가 하나 있다.

그것은 좁고 밧줄로 만들어졌다.

그들은 공원에 가기 위해 다리를 걸어서 건넌다.

그들이 다리의 중간쯤 도착했을 때, 샘이 발을 헛디딘다.

테드는 충격을 받고 소리친다. "조심해! 발걸음을 조심해!"

샘은 밧줄에 매달린다.

테드는 소리친다. "꽉 잡아."

샘은 난간으로 올라가 다리 위로 다시 기어오른다.

"아, 이 다리는 오르기에 제격이야."

다리 위에서의 그의 용감한 행동이 방송된다.

그 후, 그 다리는 세계에서 유명한 랜드마크가 된다.

Wow! Smart Vocabulary 5

워크북

WOW! Smart Grammar

전 3권 시리즈

스토리를 타고 흐르는 기본 핵심 영문법!

- ⭐ 흥미로운 스토리에 기반한 생생한 예문과 체계적인 연습문제
- ⭐ 다양한 유형의 3단계 연습문제 Quiz Time
- ⭐ 중학교 시험·공인 영어 시험 대비도 OK! Review Test
- ⭐ 부담 없이 익히는 영어권 문화 상식 Super Duper Fun Time
- ⭐ 스마트한 자기주도학습의 파트너, 워크북 & 휴대용 단어장
- ⭐ 책 속의 영어문장 해석 무료 다운로드 www.darakwon.co.kr

다락원

WOW! Smart Vocabulary 5

워크북

Unit 1
The Fortune

Word Check

A 다음 단어들의 우리말 뜻을 모두 알고 있나요? 확인해 보세요.

단어의 품사에 맞는 우리말 뜻을 쓰세요.

1. ☐ year	명		15. ☐ delivery	명		
2. ☐ dozen	명		16. ☐ maybe	부		
3. ☐ week	명		17. ☐ burglar	명		
4. ☐ mow	동		18. ☐ doorbell	명		
5. ☐ young	형		19. ☐ make angry	구		
6. ☐ hire	동		20. ☐ connect	동		
7. ☐ customer	명		21. ☐ run errands	구		
8. ☐ without	전		22. ☐ cell phone	명		
9. ☐ fortune	명		23. ☐ weak	형		
10. ☐ court	명		24. ☐ hesitate	동		
11. ☐ charity	명		25. ☐ trap	명	동	
12. ☐ blanket	명		26. ☐ invention	명		
13. ☐ homeless	형		27. ☐ earn	동		
14. ☐ nothing	대		28. ☐ millionaire	명		

B 우리말과 같은 뜻이 되도록 빈칸을 채워 영어 문장을 완성하세요.

1. 라이언 로스는 자신의 사업을 운영하는 9세 소년이다.
Ryan Ross is a 9-_____-old boy who runs his own business.

2. 3세 때, 그는 20 다스의 신선한 계란을 팔았다.
When he was three years old, he sold 20 _____ fresh eggs.

3. 그는 일주일에 약 50 달러를 벌었다.
He made about 50 dollars a _____.

4. 나중에, 그는 잔디 깎는 사업을 했다.
Later, he had a lawn-_____ business.

5. 그는 그것을 하기엔 너무 어렸다.
He was too _____ to do it.

2

6.	그래서 그는 나이가 더 많은 아이들을 고용했다.	So he ▢▢▢ older kids.
7.	그는 고객들에게 한 시간에 20 달러를 부과했다.	He charged his ▢▢▢ 20 dollars an hour.
8.	그는 아무 일도 하지 않고 한 시간에 5 달러를 벌었다.	He made 5 dollars an hour ▢▢▢ doing any work.
9.	그 후에, 그는 강력 세척사업으로 큰 돈을 벌었다.	After that, he made a ▢▢▢ in his power-washing business.
10.	그는 하키 링크와 농구장을 가지고 있다.	He has a hockey rink and a basketball ▢▢▢.
11.	그는 또한 자선 단체도 운영하고 있다.	He also runs a ▢▢▢.
12.	그는 담요들을 수집한다.	He collects ▢▢▢.
13.	그는 집 없는 사람들을 돕고 싶어한다.	He wants to help the ▢▢▢.
14.	그는 말한다."아무것도 나를 막을 수 없어요."	He says, "▢▢▢ is stopping me."
15.	테드의 엄마는 불평한다. "배달물들이 사라져 버렸어."	Ted's mom complains, "I've got some missing ▢▢▢."
16.	"아마도 누군가가 그것들을 가져갔나 봐."	"▢▢▢ somebody took them."
17.	매일, 테드는 숨어서 강도를 기다린다.	Every day, Ted hides and waits for the ▢▢▢.
18.	그는 집에 사람이 있는지 알아보기 위해 초인종을 누른다.	He rings the ▢▢▢ to see if anyone is at home.
19.	테드는 그를 약 올리고 싶다.	Ted wants to ▢▢▢ him ▢▢▢.
20.	테드는 초인종을 그의 휴대 전화에 연결한다.	Ted ▢▢▢ the ▢▢▢ to his mobile phone.
21.	테드가 심부름을 하러 외출했을 때, 그가 다시 온다.	He comes back when Ted goes out to ▢▢▢ some ▢▢▢.
22.	그가 초인종을 다시 누르고, 테드가 그의 휴대 전화를 받는다.	He rings the ▢▢▢ again, and Ted answers his ▢▢▢ ▢▢▢.
23.	테드는"나는 너무 늙고 약하다네. 들어와서 나를 좀 도와주겠나?"라고 말한다.	Ted says, "I'm so old and ▢▢▢. Can you come in and help me?"
24.	도둑은 조금 망설인다.	The thief ▢▢▢ a little.
25.	"오, 안돼!"도둑은 그물 안에 갇히고, 경찰들이 온다.	"Oh, no!" The thief is ▢▢▢ in a net, and the police officers come.
26.	사람들은 그의 영리한 발명품을 산다.	People buy his smart ▢▢▢.
27.	그는 많은 돈을 번다.	He ▢▢▢ a lot of money.
28.	그는 백만장자가 된다.	He becomes a ▢▢▢.

 빈칸에 어울리는 단어를 고르세요.

1. I take 20 classes a _____.
   ① day   ② week   ③ hour   ④ age

2. She works for a _____. She collects money from donors.
   ① school   ② restaurant   ③ charity   ④ zoo

3. My yard is a mess. I should _____ the lawn.
   ① melt   ② meet   ③ mow   ④ make

4. The _____ look for places to sleep every night.
   ① homeless   ② rich   ③ old   ④ children

5. A _____ is complaining about the price.
   ① lifesaver   ② customer   ③ court   ④ custom

6. I can't live _____ you.
   ① along   ② together   ③ without   ④ over

7. She doesn't smile at me. _____ she doesn't like me.
   ① Never   ② Finally   ③ However   ④ Maybe

8. Edison invented the light bulb. It was a great _____.
   ① invite   ② invest   ③ invention   ④ involve

9. Watch your step. There is a _____ on the ground.
   ① trip   ② trap   ③ treat   ④ try

10. A _____ donated all of his money to charity.
    ① millionaire   ② poor   ③ child   ④ million

11. Don't _____. Just do it right now.
    ① help   ② hesitate   ③ touch   ④ hurry

12. Our store promises fast _____.
    ① delivery   ② selling   ③ food   ④ delay

13. When I was watching TV, the _____ rang.
  ① window   ② couch   ③ remote control ④ doorbell

14. I _____ lots of money and bought a house.
  ① lost   ② earned   ③ broke   ④ missed

B 밑줄 친 단어와 비슷한 뜻을 가진 단어를 고르세요.

15. If you win money in the lottery, you'll make a <u>fortune</u>.
  ① health   ② luck   ③ wealth   ④ future

16. A <u>burglar</u> is breaking into the house.
  ① policeman   ② thief   ③ clerk   ④ guest

C 밑줄 친 단어와 반대되는 뜻을 가진 단어를 고르세요.

17. There is <u>nothing</u> in my pocket.
  ① zero   ② everything   ③ everybody   ④ everywhere

18. When he was <u>young</u>, he liked chocolate.
  ① pretty   ② active   ③ little   ④ old

19. I am too <u>weak</u> to lift the box.
  ① strong   ② stand   ③ strike   ④ stuck

20. The company should <u>hire</u> more people.
  ① find   ② fire   ③ get   ④ make

Score: ____ /20

Unit 2

The Bat

Word Check

A 다음 단어들의 우리말 뜻을 모두 알고 있나요? 확인해 보세요.

> 단어의 품사에 맞는 우리말 뜻을 쓰세요.

1. ☐ bat	명		15. ☐ island	명	
2. ☐ familiar	형		16. ☐ cave	명	
3. ☐ mammal	명		17. ☐ harm	동	
4. ☐ flap	동		18. ☐ ceiling	명	
5. ☐ hang	동		19. ☐ dangle	동	
6. ☐ raise	동		20. ☐ upside down	부	
7. ☐ prey	명	동	21. ☐ calm	형	
8. ☐ sound	명	동	22. ☐ shadow	명	
9. ☐ bounce	동		23. ☐ lonely	형	
10. ☐ grasp	동		24. ☐ pocket	명	형
11. ☐ death	명		25. ☐ village	명	
12. ☐ western	형		26. ☐ mouse	명	
13. ☐ however	부		27. ☐ memorial	명	
14. ☐ symbol	명		28. ☐ flier	명	

B 우리말과 같은 뜻이 되도록 빈칸을 채워 영어 문장을 완성하세요.

1.	박쥐는 전 세계 거의 모든 곳에서 발견된다.	_____ are found almost everywhere in the world.
2.	그러나 사람들은 그것들과 친밀하지 않다.	But people aren't _____ with them.
3.	그것들은 날 수 있는 유일한 포유동물이다.	They are the only _____ that can fly.
4.	그것들은 날개를 쭉 뻗어서 날갯짓을 할 수 있다.	They can _____ by spreading out their wings.
5.	그것들은 나뭇가지에 매달려서 나무에 산다.	They live in trees by _____ on the branches.

6.	동굴들은 새끼를 기르고 낮 동안 잠을 자기에 완벽한 장소들이다.	Caves are perfect places to _____ babies and to sleep during the day.
7.	그것들은 밤에 먹이를 잡을 때 자신의 귀를 이용한다.	They use their ears when they catch their _____ at night.
8.	날 때, 그것들은 약간의 소리를 낸다.	When they fly, they make some _____.
9.	그 소리들은 곤충에 부딪치고, 메아리가 다시 그것들에게 되돌아온다.	Those sounds hit insects, and the echoes _____ back to them.
10.	그것들은 빨리 날아 곤충들을 낚아챈다.	They fly fast and _____ the insects.
11.	그것들은 죽음과 관련되어 있다.	They are connected with _____.
12.	서양 문화에서 많은 사람들이 그것을 믿는다.	In _____ culture, many people believe it.
13.	그러나, 동양에서는 다르다.	_____, it is different in Asia.
14.	박쥐가 중국에서는 행복의 상징이다.	_____ are a _____ of happiness in China.
15.	테드는 섬으로 여행을 간다.	Ted takes a trip to an _____.
16.	사람들은 말한다."그 동굴에 가지 마라."	People say, "Don't go to the _____."
17.	"흡혈박쥐가 너를 잡아서 해칠 거야."	"A vampire bat will get you and _____ you."
18.	그는 천장을 올려다본다.	He looks up at the _____.
19.	무엇인가가 매달려 있다.	Something is _____.
20.	그것은 거꾸로 뒤집혀 있다.	It is _____ _____.
21.	둘 다 매우 겁을 먹었지만 차분히 가만히 있다.	Both of them are very scared but stay _____.
22.	그것은 날개를 펼쳐 큰 그림자를 만든다.	It spreads its wings and makes a big _____.
23.	그는 말한다."오, 너는 외로운 박쥐구나. 내가 네 친구가 되어줄게."	He says, "Oh, you're a _____ bat. I will be your friend."
24.	그가 그의 주머니를 열자 흡혈박쥐가 그 안으로 들어간다.	He opens his _____, and the vampire bat goes inside.
25.	그들은 마을로 내려간다.	They go down to the _____.
26.	큰 쥐들이 마을에서 사람들을 괴롭히고 물고 있다.	Big _____ are bothering and biting people in the town.
27.	그것을 기억하기 위해, 사람들은 흡혈박쥐를 위한 기념비를 세웠다.	To remember it, they built a _____ for the vampire bat.
28.	밤의 멋진 비행사	The Wonderful _____ of the Night

 빈칸에 어울리는 단어를 고르세요.

1. I prefer Korean food rather than _____ food.
   ① slow   ② Western   ③ west   ④ healthy

2. A whale is a _____.
   ① man   ② material   ③ mammal   ④ human

3. I heard the _____ of laughter.
   ① sound   ② sing   ③ soul   ④ solo

4. I get _____ money from my parents every Monday.
   ① backpack   ② pocket   ③ bag   ④ purse

5. The _____ was built by ancient people.
   ① rocket   ② label   ③ sea   ④ cave

6. When he was young, he lived in a small _____.
   ① victory   ② victim   ③ village   ④ view

7. I was _____ by my grandmother.
   ① raised   ② born   ③ mowed   ④ went

8. Lions are looking for their _____.
   ① pray   ② prayer   ③ prey   ④ player

9. She doesn't have many friends. So she feels _____.
   ① happy   ② excited   ③ fun   ④ lonely

10. People built a _____ for the dead soldiers.
    ① memory   ② memorize   ③ memo   ④ memorial

11. I will paint the _____ and walls white.
    ① ceiling   ② coin   ③ cent   ④ cell

12. Jeju _____ is well known for its beautiful scenery.
    ① land   ② Island   ③ lake   ④ load

13. An expensive car is a _____ of wealth.

① system ② syndrome ③ symbol ④ symptom

14. We heard of his _____ and felt sad.

① dean ② desk ③ death ④ dear

밑줄 친 단어와 비슷한 뜻을 가진 단어를 고르세요.

15. He studied hard. <u>However</u>, he failed the exam.

① And ② Therefore ③ So ④ But

16. When I gave the monkey a banana, the monkey <u>grasped</u> it quickly.

① grabbed ② dropped ③ threw ④ grew

17. I <u>hung</u> a picture on the wall.

① draw ② suspended ③ tore ④ took

18. Be careful! A wolf may <u>harm</u> you.

① warn ② hurt ③ hug ④ hunt

밑줄 친 단어와 반대되는 뜻을 가진 단어를 고르세요.

19. I have lived in New York for 10 years, so I am <u>familiar</u> with the city.

① well known ② unfamiliar ③ dislike ④ favor

20. He stayed <u>calm</u>. He didn't say anything.

① excited ② quiet ③ sad ④ gloomy

Score: _____ /20

Unit 2 | The Bat 9

Unit 3

Around the World

Word Check

A 다음 단어들의 우리말 뜻을 모두 알고 있나요? 확인해 보세요.

> 단어의 품사에 맞는 우리말 뜻을 쓰세요.

1.	☐ past	형 명		15.	☐ loose	형	
2.	☐ tradition	명		16.	☐ be about to	구	
3.	☐ country	명		17.	☐ wiggle	동 명	
4.	☐ receive	동		18.	☐ come out of	구	
5.	☐ bamboo	명		19.	☐ put in	구	
6.	☐ countdown	명		20.	☐ present	명 형	
7.	☐ sweet	형 명		21.	☐ crow	명	
8.	☐ festival	명		22.	☐ pillow	명	
9.	☐ fancy	형		23.	☐ couch	명	
10.	☐ calendar	명		24.	☐ fall asleep	구	
11.	☐ envelope	명		25.	☐ show up	구	
12.	☐ exchange	동 명		26.	☐ excuse	동 명	
13.	☐ firecracker	명		27.	☐ wrap	동 명	
14.	☐ delight	동 명		28.	☐ gold	형 명	

B 우리말과 같은 뜻이 되도록 빈칸을 채워 영어 문장을 완성하세요.

1.	사람들은 지난 해를 되돌아보고 새로운 해를 위한 계획을 세운다.	People look back on the _____ year and plan for the coming new year.
2.	그들은 전통들에 따라 새해를 축하한다.	They celebrate the new year with _____.
3.	그것은 그들의 나라들에서 온 것이다.	It is from their _____.
4.	일본 사람들은 새해 카드를 보내고 받으며 훈훈한 소망을 나눈다.	Japanese people send and _____ New Year's cards and share warm wishes.
5.	그들은 대나무로 집을 장식한다.	They decorate their homes with _____.

6.	멕시코에서, 사람들은 자정의 카운트다운이 시작될 때 12개의 포도 알을 먹는다.	In Mexico, people eat 12 grapes when the midnight _____ begins.
7.	각각의 달콤한 포도 알은 새해의 각 달의 행운을 나타낸다.	Each of the _____ grapes stands for good luck for each month of the new year.
8.	브라질에서 축제는 중요한 부분이다.	A _____ is an important part in Brazil.
9.	사람들은 화려한 옷을 입고 춤을 춘다.	People dance while dressed in _____ clothes.
10.	중국 사람들은 음력으로 새해를 축하한다.	Chinese people celebrate New Year's Day on the lunar _____.
11.	그들은 행운의 돈을 빨간 봉투들에 집어넣는다.	They put lucky money in red _____.
12.	그 다음, 그들은 그것들을 새해 선물로 교환한다.	Then, they _____ them as gifts for the new year.
13.	그들은 또 폭죽들을 쏘고 사자 춤을 즐긴다.	They also light _____ and enjoy lion dances.
14.	당신의 나라에서 당신을 즐겁게 하는 새해 축하에는 어떤 것이 있는가?	What New Year's Day celebration in your country _____ you?
15.	점심 때, 테드는 친구들에게 말한다. "내 이가 흔들거려."	At lunch, Ted says to his friends, "My tooth is _____."
16.	"이게 막 빠지려고 해."	"It _____ _____ _____ fall out."
17.	그는 손가락으로 자기 이를 흔든다.	He _____ his tooth with his finger.
18.	그러자, 그것이 그의 입 밖으로 나온다.	Then, it _____ _____ his mouth.
19.	스페인에서 온 마르코가 말한다. "오, 너의 이를 쥐구멍에 넣어."	Marco from Spain says, "Oh, _____ your tooth _____ a mouse hole."
20.	"이빨 쥐가 그것을 가져가고 너에게 선물을 줄 거야."	"The Tooth Mouse will take it and give you a _____."
21.	"까마귀가 그것을 가져가고 너에게 튼튼한 새 이를 줄 거야."	"A _____ will take it and give you a strong, new one."
22.	저녁을 먹은 직후에, 테드는 그의 이를 베게 밑에 놓는다.	Right after dinner, Ted puts his tooth under his _____.
23.	그는 소파에 눕는다.	He lies on the _____.
24.	그는 빠르게 잠이 든다.	He _____ _____ quickly.
25.	이의 요정 타라가 나타난다.	Tara, the Tooth Fairy, _____ _____.
26.	타라는 말한다:"실례합니다. 당신의 이를 가져가도 될까요?"	Tara says, "_____ me. Can I take your tooth?"
27.	이의 요정은 이를 종이에 싼다.	The Tooth Fairy _____ the tooth in paper.
28.	이의 요정은 테드에게 금화를 준다.	The Tooth Fairy gives _____ coins to Ted.

A 빈칸에 어울리는 단어를 고르세요.

1. I want to go to the Busan International Film _____.
   ① Fear   ② Festival   ③ Feel   ④ Fee

2. I looked at the _____ to check the date.
   ① desk   ② pencil   ③ calendar   ④ book

3. Someone asked me, "_____ me. Where is the library?"
   ① Exam   ② Expect   ③ Exit   ④ Excuse

4. Chocolates are _____ individually.
   ① wrapped   ② wrong   ③ spilled   ④ written

5. I took a rest on the _____ and watched TV.
   ① coach   ② couch   ③ cup   ④ remote control

6. There was a letter in the _____.
   ① envelope   ② environment   ③ entire   ④ encourage

7. I was _____ to hear the news.
   ① delicious   ② delay   ③ deliver   ④ delighted

8. I lived in a foreign _____ for 10 years.
   ① contact   ② container   ③ country   ④ concept

9. This is a _____ for you. Happy birthday!
   ① present   ② prefer   ③ pleasant   ④ preference

10. She lost weight, so her clothes are too _____.
    ① tight   ② small   ③ loose   ④ fit

11. She won a _____ medal at the Olympics.
    ① ground   ② gold   ③ glue   ④ goal

12. I _____ my money _____ my pocket.
    ① put, in   ② take, off   ③ put, on   ④ get, up

13. _____ is hollow but strong.

① Pine   ② Flower   ③ Bamboo   ④ Grass

14. We _____ Christmas cards.

① charged   ② endangered   ③ excited   ④ exchanged

B 밑줄 친 단어와 비슷한 뜻을 가진 단어를 고르세요.

15. Did you <u>receive</u> my mail?

① give   ② get   ③ send   ④ provide

16. Eating rice cake soup on New Year's Day is an old <u>tradition</u> in Korea.

① generation   ② appointment   ③ custom   ④ training

17. I waited for him, but he didn't <u>show up</u>.

① go out   ② run away   ③ appear   ④ disappear

C 밑줄 친 단어와 반대되는 뜻을 가진 단어를 고르세요.

18. In the <u>past</u>, women didn't have the right to vote.

① old   ② future   ③ present   ④ now

19. I bought a <u>fancy</u> dress for the dinner party.

① beautiful   ② pretty   ③ handsome   ④ plain

20. When I was a child, I liked <u>sweet</u> things.

① bitter   ② soft   ③ cold   ④ hot

Score: _____ /20

Unit 4

Life Cycle

Word Check

A 다음 단어들의 우리말 뜻을 모두 알고 있나요? 확인해 보세요.

> 단어의 품사에 맞는 우리말 뜻을 쓰세요.

1. ☐ germinate 동
2. ☐ frog 명
3. ☐ amphibian 명   형
4. ☐ lay 동
5. ☐ be covered with 구
6. ☐ hatch 동
7. ☐ tadpole 명
8. ☐ gills 명
9. ☐ lung 명
10. ☐ look like 구
11. ☐ froglet 명
12. ☐ complete 형   동
13. ☐ again 부
14. ☐ life cycle 명

15. ☐ behave 동
16. ☐ unbelievable 형
17. ☐ age 명
18. ☐ ugly 형
19. ☐ avoid 동
20. ☐ whenever 접
21. ☐ turn back 구
22. ☐ why 부
23. ☐ recognize 동
24. ☐ new 형   명
25. ☐ explain 동
26. ☐ apologize 동
27. ☐ look down on 구
28. ☐ accept 동

B 우리말과 같은 뜻이 되도록 빈칸을 채워 영어 문장을 완성하세요.

1.	봄에 씨앗이 싹트고 꽃이 핀다.	In spring, seeds _____ and flowers bloom.
2.	"개굴! 개굴!" 개구리가 연못에 있다.	"Ribbit! Ribbit" A _____ is in the pond.
3.	그것은 양서류이다.	It is an _____.
4.	그것은 물속에 많은 알을 낳는다.	It _____ many eggs in the water.
5.	그것의 알은 젤리 같은 막으로 덮여 있다.	Its eggs _____ _____ _____ a jellylike coating.

6.	약 6일에서 21일 후에, 알은 부화한다.	About 6 to 21 days later, the eggs [_____].
7.	7일에서 10일 후에, 올챙이가 헤엄을 치기 시작한다.	7 to 10 days later, a [_____] begins to swim.
8.	그것은 물속에서 아가미들로 호흡한다.	It breathes with its [_____] in the water.
9.	자라면서, 그것들은 사라지고 허파들이 만들어진다.	As it grows, they disappear, and [_____] form.
10.	약 9주 후면, 그것은 꼬리를 가진 어린 개구리처럼 보인다.	After about 9 weeks, it [_____] [_____] a young [_____] with a tail.
11.	우리는 그것을 새끼 개구리라고 부른다.	We call it a [_____].
12.	12주에서 16주까지, 개구리의 성장은 완성된다.	By 12 to 16 weeks, a [_____]'s growth is [_____].
13.	이 순환은 다시 시작된다.	This cycle begins [_____].
14.	그것의 생활 주기는 계속된다.	Its [_____] [_____] continues.
15.	7세 때, 테드는 부모님과 친구들에게 매우 무례하게 행동했다.	Ted [_____] very rudely to his parents and friends when he was 7.
16.	어느 날, 믿을 수 없는 어떤 일이 그에게 일어났다.	One day, something [_____] happened to him.
17.	그가 거울을 보았을 때, 그는 그 나이 또래의 다른 소년들보다 더 나이 들어 보였다.	When he looked in the mirror, he looked older than the other boys his [_____].
18.	"오, 안돼! 나는 너무 못생겼어! 나는 노인처럼 보여."	"Oh, no! I'm so [_____]! I look like an old man."
19.	테드는 슬퍼서 밖으로 나가는 것을 피했다.	Ted was sad, so he [_____] going outside.
20.	그가 착하게 행동할 때마다, 그는 더 어려졌다.	[_____] he acted nicely, he became younger.
21.	착한 행동은 시간을 되돌렸다.	Good behavior [_____] time.
22.	"테드, 밖에 나가서 네 친구들과 노는 것이 어떠니?" 엄마가 말했다.	"Ted, [_____] don't you go outside and play with your friends?" Mom asked.
23.	테드는 밖으로 나갔다. 그의 친구들은 그를 알아보지 못했다.	Ted went outside. His friends didn't [_____] him.
24.	"너는 누구니? 새로 온 아이니?"	"Who are you? Are you [_____]?"
25.	테드는 그에게 어떤 일이 일어났는지 설명했다.	Ted [_____] what had happened to him.
26.	테드는 친구들에게 사과했다.	Ted [_____] to his friends.
27.	"나는 전에 너희들을 업신여겼어."	"I [_____] [_____] [_____] you before."
28.	테드의 친구들은 그의 사과를 받아들이고 그와 함께 놀았다.	Ted's friends [_____] his apology and played with him.

 빈칸에 어울리는 단어를 고르세요.

1. She looks younger than her _____.
   ① year   ② age   ③ old   ④ height

2. The new leaves started to _____.
   ① spring   ② sprint   ③ speak   ④ germinate

3. I will not give up. I'll try _____.
   ① again   ② never   ③ ago   ④ ever

4. Fish breathe with their _____ underwater.
   ① gills   ② hands   ③ legs   ④ eyes

5. People don't like him, so they _____ him.
   ① follow   ② avoid   ③ respect   ④ praise

6. He _____ for keeping me waiting.
   ① suggested   ② apologized   ③ thought   ④ invited

7. I said hello to her, but she didn't _____ me.
   ① recommend   ② recover   ③ receive   ④ recognize

8. It is _____ that he broke up with his girlfriend.
   ① believe   ② understand   ③ unbelievable   ④ able

9. _____ I called her, she didn't answer.
   ① Whenever   ② Whatever   ③ However   ④ Whichever

10. The eggs need a warm place to _____.
   ① catch   ② watch   ③ hatch   ④ reach

11. Smoking can cause _____ cancer.
   ① lunar   ② lunch   ③ lung   ④ long

12. What does he _____?
   ① get up   ② take for   ③ look like   ④ go to

13. He _____ well when he was young.
   ① had   ② behaved   ③ belonged   ④ bought

14. Tell me _____ you are so angry.
   ① where   ② who   ③ what   ④ why

15. We made a _____ set for the scene.
   ① compare   ② discuss   ③ confuse   ④ complete

B 밑줄 친 단어와 비슷한 뜻을 가진 단어를 고르세요.

16. Salmon come back to river and <u>lay eggs</u>.
   ① lie   ② lean   ③ swim   ④ spawn

17. A tour guide <u>explained</u> the history of the building.
   ① described   ② excused   ③ exchanged   ④ shouted

C 밑줄 친 단어와 반대되는 뜻을 가진 단어를 고르세요.

18. I bought a <u>new</u> cell phone yesterday.
   ① good   ② fancy   ③ old   ④ cheap

19. Mike is <u>ugly</u>, but people like him.
   ① plain   ② beautiful   ③ old   ④ young

20. They <u>accepted</u> my invitation.
   ① got   ② refused   ③ received   ④ pleased

Score: _____ /20

Unit 5

Space

Word Check

A 다음 단어들의 우리말 뜻을 모두 알고 있나요? 확인해 보세요.

> 단어의 품사에 맞는 우리말 뜻을 쓰세요.

1. ☐ spacecraft （명）
2. ☐ astronaut （명）
3. ☐ moon （명）
4. ☐ near （형） （전）
5. ☐ event （명）
6. ☐ launch （동）
7. ☐ circle （동） （명）
8. ☐ alarm （명） （동）
9. ☐ data （명）
10. ☐ deal （동）
11. ☐ finally （부）
12. ☐ fine （형） （명）
13. ☐ footprint （명）
14. ☐ history （명）

15. ☐ space （명）
16. ☐ alien （명）
17. ☐ weird （형）
18. ☐ suggest （동）
19. ☐ holiday （명）
20. ☐ discuss （동）
21. ☐ spacesuit （명）
22. ☐ equipment （명）
23. ☐ hill （명）
24. ☐ telescope （명）
25. ☐ satellite （명）
26. ☐ Mars （명）
27. ☐ beg （동）
28. ☐ plate （명）

B 우리말과 같은 뜻이 되도록 빈칸을 채워 영어 문장을 완성하세요.

1. 아폴로 11호는 미국의 우주선이었다.

   Apollo 11 was an American   .

2. 세 명의 우주비행사가 1969년 7월에 아폴로 11호에 탑승했다.

   Three   were aboard *Apollo 11* in July 1969.

3. 그들에게는 달을 탐사하는 임무가 있었다.

   They were on a mission to explore the   .

4. 많은 사람들이 우주 센터 가까이에 모였다.

   Many people gathered   the space center.

5. 수백만 명의 사람들이 TV로 그 사건을 보았다.

   Millions watched the   on television.

6.	아폴로 11호를 탑재한 로켓이 발사되었다.	A rocket carrying *Apollo 11* was _____.
7.	아폴로 11호는 지구를 회전한 다음 거기로 날아갔다.	*Apollo 11* _____ the Earth and then flew there.
8.	거기에 착륙하는 동안 경보가 울렸다.	The _____ went off while landing there.
9.	컴퓨터 데이터에 문제가 있었다.	There was trouble with the computer _____.
10.	그러나 우주비행사들이 침착하게 문제를 해결했다.	But the _____ _____ with the problem calmly.
11.	그들은 마침내 착륙했다.	They _____ landed.
12.	그 표면은 미세한 먼지로 뒤덮여 있었다.	The surface was covered with a _____ powder.
13.	그들은 그곳에 첫 발자국들을 남겼다.	They left the first _____ there.
14.	그 행성으로 가는 여행의 역사는 아폴로 11호와 시작되었다.	The _____ of travel to the planet began with *Apollo 11*.
15.	테드는 우주에 관한 이야기에 흠뻑 빠져 있다.	Ted is really into stories about _____.
16.	그는 외계인들을 만나고 싶다.	He hopes to meet _____.
17.	그러나 모두 그의 이상한 생각을 비웃는다.	But everybody laughs at his _____ ideas.
18.	타라가 아이디어 하나를 제안한다.	Tara _____ an idea.
19.	그것은 우주에서 여름 방학을 보내는 것이다.	It is spending the summer _____ in _____.
20.	그들은 여행에 대한 계획을 논의한다.	They _____ their plans for the trip.
21.	"우리는 우주복, 음식, 그리고 카메라가 필요해."	"We need _____, food, and a camera."
22.	그들은 여행에 필요한 모든 장비를 준비한다.	They get all the _____ ready for the trip.
23.	그들은 언덕으로 올라간다.	They go up the _____.
24.	그들은 망원경으로 하늘을 올려다본다.	They look up at the sky through a _____.
25.	테드가 인공위성 라디오를 켠다.	Ted turns on the _____ radio.
26.	"나는 화성에서 온 세비야."	"I'm Sevi from _____."
27.	테드와 타라는 그녀에게 애원한다.	Ted and Tara _____ her.
28.	UFO는 나는 접시처럼 생겼다.	The UFO is like a flying _____.

Ⓐ 빈칸에 어울리는 단어를 고르세요.

1. The sun rises in the daytime, and the _____ rises at night.
   ① moon   ② mood   ③ move   ④ model

2. You can see the sun without a _____.
   ① telescope   ② television   ③ telegraph   ④ telephone

3. Let's survey and make a graph of the _____.
   ① date   ② dark   ③ duet   ④ data

4. This Wednesday is a _____ because it's New Year's Day.
   ① hope   ② holiday   ③ help   ④ honor

5. Cinderella's sisters tried to stop her, but she _____ met the prince.
   ① final   ② fine   ③ finally   ④ fire

6. The Korean government decided to send medical _____ to the devastated area.
   ① equip   ② envelope   ③ equipment   ④ eraser

7. I want to be an _____. I will visit Venus.
   ① agent   ② astronaut   ③ astrology   ④ address

8. Navigation is controlled by a _____.
   ① satellite   ② spell   ③ sail   ④ strip

9. There is a _____ on the ground.
   ① footage   ② footing   ③ footnote   ④ footprint

10. Some people believe that _____ exist.
    ① airports   ② aliens   ③ adults   ④ alternatives

11. You need to learn how to _____ with your problems.
    ① dry   ② draw   ③ deal   ④ destroy

12. They failed to _____ the rocket.

① laugh   ② launch   ③ lose   ④ laundry

13. The poor boys _____ for money from people at the movie.

① became   ② broke   ③ begged   ④ began

14. NASA developed a new _____ with advanced technology.

① spacecraft   ② airspace   ③ space time   ④ space age

B 밑줄 친 단어와 비슷한 뜻을 가진 단어를 고르세요.

15. I like science, but I don't like the <u>history</u> of science.

① check   ② chronicle   ③ charge   ④ challenge

16. We are going to <u>discuss</u> about wearing school uniforms.

① defeat   ② decline   ③ decide   ④ debate

17. Pass me your <u>plate</u>, and I'll give you some food.

① dash   ② dress   ③ dish   ④ dust

18. The vet <u>suggests</u> that I walk my dog every day.

① supplies   ② introduces   ③ produces   ④ proposes

C 밑줄 친 단어와 반대되는 뜻을 가진 단어를 고르세요.

19. Our school is very <u>near</u>.

① for   ② fur   ③ far   ④ fall

20. Sometimes, my classmates are <u>weird</u>. They yell or run in the classroom.

① normal   ② noise   ③ northern   ④ normally

Score: _____ /20

Unit 6

The Ocean

Word Check

A 다음 단어들의 우리말 뜻을 모두 알고 있나요? 확인해 보세요.

단어의 품사에 맞는 우리말 뜻을 쓰세요.

1. ☐ stream (명) (동)
2. ☐ salmon (명)
3. ☐ migration (명)
4. ☐ salt (명) (형) (동)
5. ☐ enter (동)
6. ☐ adult (명) (형)
7. ☐ fail (동)
8. ☐ survive (동)
9. ☐ several (형)
10. ☐ return (동)
11. ☐ instinct (명)
12. ☐ rock (명) (동)
13. ☐ female (형) (명)
14. ☐ male (형) (명)

15. ☐ cruise (명) (동)
16. ☐ captain (명)
17. ☐ pirate (명)
18. ☐ area (명)
19. ☐ often (부)
20. ☐ ship (명)
21. ☐ terrible (형)
22. ☐ sweep (동)
23. ☐ take over (구)
24. ☐ threaten (동)
25. ☐ passenger (명)
26. ☐ treasure (명)
27. ☐ search (동) (명)
28. ☐ away (부)

B 우리말과 같은 뜻이 되도록 빈칸을 채워 영어 문장을 완성하세요.

1. 여기 차갑고 맑은 개울이 있다. Here is a cold and clear _____.

2. 아주 작은 아기 연어들이 민물에서 수영한다. Some tiny baby _____ swim in the fresh water.

3. 그들은 바다로 이주를 시작한다. They start their _____ to the ocean.

4. 그들의 몸은 바닷물에서 살 수 있게끔 변한다. Their bodies change to live in _____ water.

5. 마침내, 그들은 바다에 들어간다. At last, they _____ the ocean.

6.	그들은 바다에서 어른 연어들로 자란다.	They grow into [____] salmon in the ocean.
7.	그들 중 일부는 큰 바다에서 사는 데 실패한다.	Some of them [____] to live in the big ocean.
8.	그들 중 단지 몇몇만 바닷물고기 사이에서 살아남는다.	Only a few of them [____] among the saltwater fish.
9.	그들은 여러 해 후에 바다를 떠난다.	They leave the ocean after [____] years.
10.	그들은 그들의 개울로 다시 돌아가기 위해 노력한다.	They try to [____] to their stream.
11.	그들은 고향으로 돌아가려는 본능이 있다.	They have the [____] to go back home.
12.	도착한 후에, 연어들은 바위 사이에 알을 낳는다.	After arriving, the salmon lay eggs among the [____].
13.	암컷 연어들은 수천 개의 알을 낳는다.	[____] salmon lay thousands of eggs.
14.	수컷 연어들은 그들을 돕는다.	[____] salmon help them.
15.	테드는 가족들과 함께 유람선 여행을 한다.	Ted takes a [____] with his family.
16.	테드가 선장에게 묻는다.	Ted asks the [____].
17.	"우리가 해적들을 볼 기회가 있을까요?"	"Will we have a chance to see any [____]?"
18.	그가 대답한다. "글쎄요, 서쪽이 위험한 지역이에요."	He answers, "Well, the west side is the dangerous [____]."
19.	"그들이 가끔 그곳을 항해하죠."	"They [____] sail there."
20.	테드는 고요한 바다에 있는 배에서 즐거움을 만끽한다.	Ted has fun on the [____] in the calm ocean.
21.	그날 밤, 지독한 폭풍이 몰아친다.	That night, a [____] storm blows.
22.	배가 바다의 서쪽으로 쓸려간다.	The [____] is [____] to the west side of the ocean.
23.	아침에 무서운 공격자들이 그것을 차지한다.	In the morning, scary attackers [____] [____] it.
24.	그러고 나서 그들은 사람들을 협박한다.	Then they [____] people.
25.	테드가 그들에게 소리 지른다. "승객들 중에 왕자가 있어요."	Ted shouts at them, "There is a prince among the [____]."
26.	"그는 침대 밑에 커다란 보물 상자를 가지고 있죠."	"He has a big [____] chest under his bed."
27.	그들은 상자를 찾는다.	They [____] for the chest.
28.	테드와 다른 사람들은 해적들의 배를 타고 달아난다.	Ted and the other people take the [____]' ship and sail [____].

Ⓐ 빈칸에 어울리는 단어를 고르세요.

1. The sand is softer than the _____ .
   ① roles   ② royal   ③ rocks   ④ rate

2. This _____ is a dangerous place to play alone.
   ① area   ② around   ③ article   ④ address

3. When I become an _____ , I want to be like my father.
   ① adopt   ② adult   ③ admit   ④ advice

4. The _____ makes the workers clean the ship.
   ① capital   ② capture   ③ calm   ④ captain

5. Don't be disappointed. You won't _____ next time.
   ① fall   ② foil   ③ feel   ④ fail

6. When the floor is dirty, _____ the floor, please.
   ① switch   ② swear   ③ sweep   ④ sweet

7. I told her to finish her homework before lunch _____ times.
   ① seventh   ② survey   ③ several   ④ sense

8. The number one National _____ in Korea is Namdaemun.
   ① Tradition   ② Treaty   ③ Treatment   ④ Treasure

9. Bird _____ is an interesting part of nature.
   ① migration   ② million   ③ military   ④ mind

10. The _____ took a lot of jewelry from the ship.
    ① parade   ② pirate   ③ paradise   ④ period

11. An animal's natural _____ is to survive.
    ① instead   ② install   ③ insist   ④ instinct

12. The police _____ for the missing child.
    ① search   ② serious   ③ server   ④ servant

13. He was lucky to _____ the car accident.

① surround   ② surprise   ③ survive   ④ surface

14. Attention, _____. This is an emergency. Get off the train.

① passengers   ② passports   ③ passwords   ④ passion

15. Another company will _____ our company next month.

① take over   ② take out   ③ take in   ④ take from

B 밑줄 친 단어와 비슷한 뜻을 가진 단어를 고르세요.

16. People <u>often</u> make mistakes.

① freeze   ② frequently   ③ freedom   ④ frustrate

17. Teenage runaways should <u>return</u> to their homes.

① come before   ② come up   ③ come back   ④ come between

18. It is <u>terrible</u> to work alone at night.

① wonderful   ② amazing   ③ fantastic   ④ horrible

C 밑줄 친 단어와 반대되는 뜻을 가진 단어를 고르세요.

19. Don't <u>enter</u> this shopping mall. There is a bomb.

① exist   ② exit   ③ explain   ④ expect

20. <u>Female</u> animals lay eggs or give birth to their babies.

① Mail   ② Mall   ③ Male   ④ Matter

Score: _____ /20

Unit 7
Great Adventures

Word Check

A 다음 단어들의 우리말 뜻을 모두 알고 있나요? 확인해 보세요.

> 단어의 품사에 맞는 우리말 뜻을 쓰세요.

1. ☐ polar 〈형〉		15. ☐ theater 〈명〉	
2. ☐ expedition 〈명〉		16. ☐ triangle 〈명〉	
3. ☐ succeed 〈동〉		17. ☐ daughter 〈명〉	
4. ☐ attempt 〈동〉 〈명〉		18. ☐ reason 〈명〉	
5. ☐ shore 〈명〉		19. ☐ screen 〈명〉	
6. ☐ prepare 〈동〉		20. ☐ submarine 〈명〉	
7. ☐ vehicle 〈명〉		21. ☐ whirlpool 〈명〉	
8. ☐ the English 〈구〉		22. ☐ draw into 〈구〉	
9. ☐ exhausted 〈형〉		23. ☐ bubble 〈명〉 〈동〉	
10. ☐ suffer 〈동〉		24. ☐ get worse 〈구〉	
11. ☐ frostbite 〈명〉 〈동〉		25. ☐ situation 〈명〉	
12. ☐ run out of 〈구〉		26. ☐ press 〈동〉 〈명〉	
13. ☐ a few 〈구〉		27. ☐ bacteria 〈명〉	
14. ☐ national 〈형〉		28. ☐ hero 〈명〉	

B 우리말과 같은 뜻이 되도록 빈칸을 채워 영어 문장을 완성하세요.

1.	극지의 모험은 19세기에 시작되었다.	The _____ adventure began in the nineteenth century.
2.	1912년 이전에 많은 탐험대들이 남극에 도달하고자 애썼다.	Many _____ had tried to reach the South Pole before 1912.
3.	하지만 어느 누구도 남극에 도달하는 데 성공하지 못했다.	But nobody _____ at getting to the South Pole.
4.	로버트 스캇의 팀이 남극에 처음으로 도착하고자 시도했다.	Robert Scott's team _____ to be the first to get to the South Pole.
5.	그들은 해안가에 베이스 캠프를 차렸다.	They set up a base camp on the _____.

26

6.	그들은 신중하게 준비했다.	They carefully ⬚⬚⬚⬚⬚.
7.	그들은 개 썰매, 조랑말과 탈것들을 가지고 갔다.	They took sled dogs, ponies, and ⬚⬚⬚⬚⬚.
8.	노르웨이 사람들이 영국 사람들보다 5주 전에 먼저 남극에 도착했다.	The Norwegians reached the South Pole 5 weeks before ⬚⬚⬚ ⬚⬚⬚.
9.	그들은 매우 실망했고 기진맥진했다.	They were very disappointed and ⬚⬚⬚⬚⬚.
10.	그들은 돌아오는 길에 악천후로 고생했다.	They ⬚⬚⬚⬚⬚ from the bad weather on their way back.
11.	그들은 아팠고, 동상에 걸렸다.	They became ill and got ⬚⬚⬚⬚⬚.
12.	그들은 음식이 다 떨어져서 굶어 죽었다.	They ⬚⬚⬚ ⬚⬚⬚ ⬚⬚⬚ food and died of hunger.
13.	그들은 그들의 베이스 캠프로부터 몇 킬로미터 떨어진 곳에서 발견되었다.	They were found ⬚⬚⬚ ⬚⬚⬚ kilometers from their base camp.
14.	그들은 실패했지만 국가의 영웅들이 되었다.	They failed but became ⬚⬚⬚⬚⬚ heroes.
15.	테드는 극장에서 영화를 봤다.	Ted watched a movie at the ⬚⬚⬚⬚⬚.
16.	마의 삼각 지대에 관한 모험영화였다.	It was an adventure film about the Devil's ⬚⬚⬚⬚⬚.
17.	한 과학자가 거기에서 그녀의 딸을 잃어버렸다.	A scientist lost her ⬚⬚⬚⬚⬚ there.
18.	테드는 "나는 그들이 사라진 이유를 밝혀내고 싶어"라고 말한다.	Ted says, "I want to discover the ⬚⬚⬚⬚⬚ they went missing."
19.	그때, 테드는 화면 속으로 들어간다.	At that moment, Ted falls into the ⬚⬚⬚⬚⬚.
20.	테드와 과학자가 잠수함을 타고 탐험을 떠난다.	Ted and a scientist get in a ⬚⬚⬚⬚⬚ and go on an ⬚⬚⬚⬚⬚.
21.	갑자기, 그 장소 근처에서 소용돌이가 생겨난다.	Suddenly, a ⬚⬚⬚⬚⬚ forms near the place.
22.	잠수함이 구멍 안으로 끌려 들어간다.	The ⬚⬚⬚⬚⬚ is ⬚⬚⬚⬚⬚ the hole.
23.	바다 바닥으로부터 공기 거품이 올라온다.	Gas ⬚⬚⬚⬚⬚ up from the bottom of the sea.
24.	테드가 소리친다. "점점 심해져요."	Ted shouts, "It is ⬚⬚⬚ ⬚⬚⬚."
25.	"상황이 매우 나빠요."	"The ⬚⬚⬚⬚⬚ is very bad."
26.	과학자가 버튼을 누른다.	The scientist ⬚⬚⬚⬚⬚ a button.
27.	그러자 많은 세균들이 나와서 공기 거품들을 잡는다.	Then, a lot of ⬚⬚⬚⬚⬚ come out and catch the gas ⬚⬚⬚⬚⬚.
28.	그들은 그 장소의 수수께끼를 풀고 영웅들이 된다.	They solve the mystery of the place and become ⬚⬚⬚⬚⬚.

A 빈칸에 어울리는 단어를 고르세요.

1. They plan an _____ to Mt. Everest.
   ① expedition   ② expectation   ③ explain   ④ vehicle

2. Many people _____ because of the earthquakes.
   ① enjoyed   ② suffered   ③ tested   ④ watched

3. When I was lost in the forest last winter, I got _____.
   ① front   ② heat   ③ screen   ④ frostbite

4. He _____ gas, so he had to walk.
   ① ran   ② drew into   ③ ran out of   ④ exhausted

5. Will you help me _____ for her birthday party?
   ① succeed   ② get worse   ③ prepare   ④ attempt

6. After she finished the marathon, she was _____.
   ① exciting   ② exhausted   ③ triangle   ④ scary

7. I could not watch the movie in the _____.
   ① theater   ② stage   ③ polar   ④ picture

8. She was late for no _____.
   ① whirlpool   ② reason   ③ way   ④ bubble

9. They saw stars being _____ a black hole in space.
   ① get to   ② driven into   ③ drawing   ④ drawn into

10. We can go on a trip under the sea in a _____.
    ① subway   ② sunshine   ③ submarine   ④ subject

11. We expect the _____ soccer team will win the game.
    ① national   ② nation   ③ native   ④ bubble

12. If you win the game, you will be a _____.
    ① doctor   ② hero   ③ teacher   ④ daughter

13. When he took the elevator, he _____ button number 5.

   ① pulled   ② printed   ③ wrote   ④ pressed

14. I read _____ books this summer.

   ① much   ② a few   ③ little   ④ a little

15. His grandparents have one son and two _____.

   ① daughters   ② grandson   ③ cat   ④ uncle

B 밑줄 친 단어와 비슷한 뜻을 가진 단어를 고르세요.

16. Let's take a walk along the <u>shore</u>.

   ① lake   ② park   ③ coast   ④ street

17. They <u>attempted</u> to escape from a shark.

   ① survived   ② tried   ③ gave up   ④ jumped

18. The Korean economic <u>situation</u> is good these days.

   ① test   ② growth   ③ condition   ④ policy

C 밑줄 친 단어와 반대되는 뜻을 가진 단어를 고르세요.

19. My dog has been sick for three days. He's <u>getting worse</u>.

   ① getting hungry   ② getting better   ③ getting late   ④ getting bored

20. I finally <u>succeeded</u> at passing the test.

   ① fell   ② made   ③ followed   ④ failed

Score: _____/20

The Honor

Word Check

A 다음 단어들의 우리말 뜻을 모두 알고 있나요? 확인해 보세요.

> 단어의 품사에 맞는 우리말 뜻을 쓰세요.

1. ☐ international	형		15. ☐ know	동	
2. ☐ corner	명		16. ☐ dictionary	명	
3. ☐ honor	동	명	17. ☐ participate	동	
4. ☐ physics	명		18. ☐ advance	동	명
5. ☐ literature	명		19. ☐ confident	형	
6. ☐ establish	동		20. ☐ competition	명	
7. ☐ be noted for	구		21. ☐ everybody	대	
8. ☐ wealth	명		22. ☐ mistake	명	
9. ☐ since	접		23. ☐ chance	명	
10. ☐ consist	동		24. ☐ question	명	동
11. ☐ cash	명		25. ☐ bloat	동	
12. ☐ ceremony	명		26. ☐ break wind	구	
13. ☐ anniversary	명		27. ☐ giggle	동	
14. ☐ more than	구		28. ☐ correct	형	

B 우리말과 같은 뜻이 되도록 빈칸을 채워 영어 문장을 완성하세요.

1.	노벨상은 국제적인 상이다.	The Nobel Prize is an ▢ award.
2.	이 상은 세계 각지의 사람들에게 수여한다.	It awards people from all ▢ of the world.
3.	이것은 매년 여섯 개의 다른 분야에서 최고의 업적을 이룬 사람들에게 영예를 준다.	It ▢ the people who did the best work in six different fields each year.
4.	그것들은 물리학, 화학, 약학 분야이다.	They are ▢, chemistry, and medicine.
5.	다른 분야는 문학과 경제학, 세계 평화 분야이다.	The others are ▢, economic sciences, and work for world peace.

6.	알프레드 노벨이 이 상을 설립했다.	Alfred Nobel _____ the prize.
7.	그는 다이너마이트 발명으로 유명하다.	He _____ _____ _____ his invention of dynamite.
8.	그는 노벨상을 설립하기 위해 많은 재산을 남겼다.	He left much of his _____ to set up the Nobel Prize.
9.	노벨상은 1901년 이래로 계속 수여되고 있다.	The Nobel Prize has been awarded _____ 1901.
10.	모든 상은 증서와 메달로 구성된다.	Every prize _____ of a diploma and a medal.
11.	또한 상금도 있다.	There are also _____ awards.
12.	상 수여식은 스웨덴과 노르웨이에서 열린다.	The awards _____ are held in Sweden and Norway.
13.	수여식은 노벨의 기일인 12월 10일이다.	They are on December 10, the _____ of Nobel's death.
14.	지금까지 800명 이상의 사람들이 상을 받았다.	_____ _____ 800 people have received prizes so far.
15.	테드는 많은 단어를 알고 있고 어려운 단어들의 뜻을 찾는 것을 좋아한다.	Ted _____ many words and likes to find the meanings of difficult words.
16.	매일, 그는 많은 책들과 사전을 읽는다.	Every day, he reads many books and the _____.
17.	어느 날, 그는 철자법 대회에 참가한다.	One day, he _____ in a spelling bee.
18.	테드와 한 소녀가 결승에 나간다.	Ted and a girl _____ to the final round.
19.	그 소녀는 매우 총명하고 자신감 넘쳐 보인다.	The girl looks very smart and _____.
20.	"내가 이 대회의 우승자가 될 거야." 라고 그녀는 말한다.	She says, "I will be the winner of this _____."
21.	거의 모든 사람들이 그녀가 우승할 거라고 기대한다.	Almost _____ expects her to win.
22.	그러나 그녀는 헷갈려서 실수를 한다.	But she gets confused and makes a _____.
23.	대회 진행자가 말한다."이제 당신의 기회입니다, 테드."	The host says, "Now it's your _____, Ted."
24.	그는 마지막 질문을 테드에게 한다.	He asks the final _____ to Ted.
25.	테드는 배가 터질 것 같아서 대답을 할 수 없다.	Ted feels _____ and can't answer.
26.	갑자기, 그는 아주 크게 방귀를 뀐다.	Suddenly, he _____ _____ very loudly.
27.	사람들이 낄낄 웃기 시작해서 테드는 긴장한다.	People start to _____, so Ted feels nervous.
28.	"와우, 정답입니다! 당신이 철자법 대회의 웃긴 우승자네요."	"Wow, that's _____! You are the funny winner of the spelling bee."

 빈칸에 어울리는 단어를 고르세요.

1. This town _____ its fine view.
   ① begins   ② is big   ③ gets correct   ④ is noted for

2. Go straight and take a left at the _____.
   ① question   ② corner   ③ dictionary   ④ cash

3. We have known each other _____ 2010.
   ① in   ② by   ③ for   ④ since

4. I am interested in _____ like Einstein.
   ① cash   ② ceremony   ③ physics   ④ cruise

5. We have to _____ a new tradition for our children.
   ① succeed   ② compete   ③ establish   ④ break wind

6. When you want to know a word's meaning, you can use a _____.
   ① telephone   ② dictionary   ③ question   ④ literature

7. Our nation gives every student a _____ to study.
   ① chase   ② cancel   ③ correct   ④ chance

8. He took me to the opening _____ of the World Cup.
   ① ceremony   ② advance   ③ mistake   ④ honor

9. She received an _____ for being the best actress.
   ① famous   ② competition   ③ honor   ④ giggle

10. I am full because I ate _____ three potatoes.
    ① a few   ② more than   ③ a little   ④ less than

11. When the actor fell down the stairs in the movie, everybody _____.
    ① mowed   ② gave up   ③ raised   ④ giggled

12. If your answer is _____, you will be the winner.
   ① correct   ② wrong   ③ short   ④ difficult

13. The baby _____ after drinking some milk.
   ① ran   ② jumped   ③ knew   ④ broke wind

14. I am interested in _____, so I like to read books.
   ① math   ② science   ③ literature   ④ music

15. She was angry because he forgot their wedding _____.
   ① people   ② anniversary   ③ aunt   ④ advance

B 밑줄 친 단어와 비슷한 뜻을 가진 단어를 고르세요.

16. The <u>international</u> festival was canceled because of the weather.
   ① global   ② earth   ③ local   ④ national

17. The soccer team <u>consists of</u> one coach and eleven players.
   ① makes   ② receives   ③ is made of   ④ bloats

18. The national baseball team can't <u>participate</u> in the competition.
   ① take part   ② get   ③ play   ④ win

C 밑줄 친 단어와 반대되는 뜻을 가진 단어를 고르세요.

19. I am <u>confident</u> that we will win the next game.
   ① difficult   ② unsure   ③ different   ④ dislike

20. His <u>wealth</u> came from a lot of hard work.
   ① protection   ② practice   ③ fortune   ④ poverty

Score: _____ /20

Step Back in Time

Word Check

A 다음 단어들의 우리말 뜻을 모두 알고 있나요? 확인해 보세요.

> 단어의 품사에 맞는 우리말 뜻을 쓰세요.

1. ☐ shop	명 동	15. ☐ clock	명
2. ☐ bath	명	16. ☐ point	동 명
3. ☐ mountain	명	17. ☐ set	동 명
4. ☐ erupt	동	18. ☐ spin	동
5. ☐ volcano	명	19. ☐ faint	동
6. ☐ ash	명	20. ☐ surround	동
7. ☐ bury	동	21. ☐ Stone Age	명
8. ☐ disaster	명	22. ☐ tool	명
9. ☐ later	부	23. ☐ sharp	형
10. ☐ uncover	동	24. ☐ edge	명
11. ☐ archaeologist	명	25. ☐ knife	명
12. ☐ petrify	동	26. ☐ wonder	동 형
13. ☐ preserve	동	27. ☐ raw	형
14. ☐ remain	동	28. ☐ create	동

B 우리말과 같은 뜻이 되도록 빈칸을 채워 영어 문장을 완성하세요.

1.	폼페이에는 큰 시장과 극장, 그리고 많은 가게들이 있었다.	Pompeii had a large market, a theater, and many _____.
2.	많은 사람들은 폼페이에서 목욕을 하고 휴식을 취하기를 즐겼다.	Many people enjoyed taking _____ and relaxing in Pompeii.
3.	산 하나가 도시 근처에 있었다.	A _____ was near the city.
4.	어느 날, 그것이 분출했다.	One day, it _____.
5.	다시 말해서, 화산이 폭발했다.	In other words, a _____ exploded.

6.	가스, 화산재, 그리고 바위들이 도시를 뒤덮었다.	Gas, _____, and rocks covered the city.
7.	폼페이는 화산 분출에 의해 빠르게 파묻혔다.	Pompeii was quickly _____ by the volcanic eruption.
8.	폼페이의 재난은 잊혀졌다.	The _____ of Pompeii was forgotten.
9.	1700년이 지나, 사람들은 잃어버린 도시 폼페이를 찾아냈다.	1,700 years _____, people found the lost city of Pompeii.
10.	그들은 로마의 그림 몇 점을 발견했다.	They _____ some Roman paintings.
11.	고고학자들이 와서 그 도시의 유적들을 파헤쳤다.	_____ came and dug up the ruins of the city.
12.	사람과 동물의 석화된 사체들이 많이 발견되었다.	A lot of _____ bodies of people and animals were discovered.
13.	그것들은 화산재와 진흙에 의해 잘 보존되었다.	They were _____ well by the ash and mud.
14.	놀랍게도, 몇몇 건축물과 집, 그리고 거리들이 남아 있었다.	Surprisingly, some buildings, houses, and streets _____.
15.	테드는 아침에 시계를 본다.	Ted looks at the _____ in the morning.
16.	그것이 멈추어서 숫자 12를 가리킨다.	It stops and _____ at 12.
17.	그는 그것을 맞추기 위해 노력한다.	He tries to _____ it.
18.	하지만 그것이 갑자기 거꾸로 돌아간다.	But it suddenly _____ back.
19.	테드는 어지러움을 느끼며 기절한다.	Ted feels dizzy and _____.
20.	그가 깨어났을 때, 그는 사람들에 의해 둘러싸여 있다.	When he wakes up, he is _____ by people.
21.	그들은 동물 가죽을 입고 있기 때문에 석기 시대에서 온 사람들 같아 보인다.	They look like people from the _____ _____ because they are wearing animal skins.
22.	남자들은 돌로 된 도구들을 갖고 사냥하러 간다.	The men go hunting with stone _____.
23.	그러나 그것들은 날카롭지 않다.	But they are not _____.
24.	테드는 돌의 가장자리를 부숴 날카롭게 만든다.	Ted breaks and sharpens the _____ of a stone.
25.	그것은 날카로운 돌칼이 된다.	It becomes a _____ stone _____.
26.	사람들은 테드를 보며 그가 어디에서 왔는지 궁금해한다.	People look at Ted and _____ where he came from.
27.	테드는 말한다."기다려요! 날 고기를 먹지 말아요."	Ted says, "Wait! Don't eat _____ meat."
28.	사람들은 소리친다."당신이 불을 만들었어요! 당신은 우리의 왕이에요!"	People shout, "You _____ fire! You're our king!"

A 빈칸에 어울리는 단어를 고르세요.

1. You should take a _____ straight after working out.
① board   ② bath   ③ bed   ④ birth

2. Mt. Fuji is an active _____.
① volume   ② volcano   ③ view   ④ volunteer

3. A flood is one kind of natural _____.
① disappoint   ② disappear   ③ direction   ④ disaster

4. She _____ the dead dog's body.
① builds   ② varies   ③ buries   ④ votes

5. The _____ has studied the volcano since 1972.
① architect   ② archaeologist   ③ artist   ④ announcer

6. The cuckoo _____ in the living room chimes every hour.
① clothes   ② clue   ③ clock   ④ clerk

7. The lake is _____ by mountains.
① surrounded   ② surfaced   ③ supplied   ④ slept

8. She sits on the _____ of the table.
① express   ② eraser   ③ edge   ④ egg

9. The new construction plan will _____ more jobs.
① cry   ② cross   ③ cream   ④ create

10. In a running race, they say, "Ready. _____. Go!"
① Sent   ② Set   ③ Send   ④ Sell

11. I'm _____ if you can come tomorrow or not.
① wondering   ② winning   ③ working   ④ wandering

12. I don't know why he is _____ at me.
① pointing   ② participating   ③ painting   ④ poisoning

13. They eat with a fork and _____.

    ① knob   ② knee   ③ knit   ④ knife

14. Do you like hiking up _____?

    ① mountains   ② moments   ③ models   ④ moving

15. Clouds of _____ cover the sky.

    ① action   ② aspect   ③ ash   ④ asking

16. She _____ the bottle, and the next person picks the card.

    ① says   ② steals   ③ sits   ④ spins

B 밑줄 친 단어와 비슷한 뜻을 가진 단어를 고르세요.

17. The <u>shop</u> is closed on Sundays.

    ① stone   ② state   ③ store   ④ storm

18. He likes to eat <u>raw</u> fish.

    ① unfolded   ② uncooked   ③ uncovered   ④ unlocked

C 밑줄 친 단어와 반대되는 뜻을 가진 단어를 고르세요.

19. Let's try to <u>uncover</u> the truth.

    ① consist   ② complain   ③ contact   ④ cover

20. I'll see you at the library <u>later</u>.

    ① in time   ② next   ③ after   ④ earlier

Score: _____ /20

Unit 10

World Landmark

Word Check

A 다음 단어들의 우리말 뜻을 모두 알고 있나요? 확인해 보세요.

단어의 품사에 맞는 우리말 뜻을 쓰세요.

1. ☐ bell ⑲	15. ☐ early ㉑
2. ☐ belong ⑧	16. ☐ neighbor ⑲
3. ☐ marble ⑲	17. ☐ steep ㉗
4. ☐ vertical ㉗	18. ☐ beside ㉓
5. ☐ construction ⑲	19. ☐ bridge ⑲
6. ☐ lean ⑧	20. ☐ rope ⑲
7. ☐ unstable ㉗	21. ☐ walk across ㉢
8. ☐ effort ⑲	22. ☐ miss one's step ㉢
9. ☐ cease ⑧	23. ☐ shock ⑧　⑲
10. ☐ foundation ⑲	24. ☐ mind one's step ㉢
11. ☐ finish ⑧	25. ☐ tight ㉗　㉑
12. ☐ degree ⑲	26. ☐ guardrail ⑲
13. ☐ even though ㉕	27. ☐ on air ㉢
14. ☐ remarkable ㉗	28. ☐ landmark ⑲

B 우리말과 같은 뜻이 되도록 빈칸을 채워 영어 문장을 완성하세요.

1.	피사의 사탑은 이탈리아의 도시 피사에 있는 유명한 종탑이다.	The Leaning Tower of Pisa is a famous _____ tower in the Italian city of Pisa.
2.	그 탑은 피사의 교회에 소속되어 있다.	The tower _____ to the church of Pisa.
3.	그것은 흰 대리석으로 덮여 있는 8층 짜리이다.	It has 8 stories covered in white _____.
4.	그것은 원래 수직으로 디자인되었다.	It was originally designed to be _____.
5.	그러나 1178년에 3층을 건설한 이후에 내려앉기 시작했다.	But it began to sink after _____ on the third floor in 1178.

6.	왜 그 탑이 내려앉고 기울어졌을까?	Why did the tower sink and ?
7.	탑은 약하고 불안정한 땅 위에 지어졌다.	The tower was built on weak, ground.
8.	건축가들은 그것이 내려앉는 것을 멈추기 위해 노력했다.	The builders made an to stop it from sinking.
9.	몇 번의 시도 후에, 그들은 100년 동안 탑 짓는 것을 중단했다.	After several attempts, they building the tower for a century.
10.	기반이 더 안정되었을 때, 그것은 다시 지어졌다.	When the became more stable, it was built again.
11.	그들은 탑 짓기를 끝마쳤고 200년 후에 다섯 층을 더 지었다.	They building the tower and added five more floors 200 years later.
12.	그것은 현재 약 3.99도 정도의 각도로 기울어져 있다.	It at an angle of about 3.99 now.
13.	비록 기울어져 있지만, 그것은 매력적으로 보인다.	it , it looks attractive.
14.	많은 관광객들이 이 놀라운 탑을 방문해서 사진을 찍는다.	Many tourists visit this tower and take pictures.
15.	테드는 아침 일찍 집을 떠난다.	Ted leaves home in the morning.
16.	그는 이웃인 샘과 소풍을 간다.	He goes on a picnic with his Sam.
17.	샘은 가파른 벽에 오르는 것을 잘한다.	Sam is good at climbing walls.
18.	그들은 공원 옆의 넓은 강에 도착한다.	They arrive at a wide river a park.
19.	강 위에는 다리가 하나 있다.	There's a over the river.
20.	그것은 좁고 밧줄로 만들어졌다.	It is narrow and made of .
21.	그들은 공원에 가기 위해 그것을 걸어서 건넌다.	They it to get to the park.
22.	그들이 다리의 중간쯤 도착했을 때, 샘은 발을 헛디딘다.	When they reach the middle of the bridge, Sam .
23.	테드는 충격을 받고 소리친다.	Ted is and shouts.
24.	"조심해! 발걸음을 조심해!"	"Watch out! !"
25.	테드는 소리친다."꽉 잡아."	Ted shouts, "Hold on ."
26.	샘은 난간으로 올라온다.	Sam moves up the .
27.	다리 위에서의 그의 용감한 행동이 방송된다.	His brave act on the bridge is put .
28.	그 후, 그 다리는 세계에서 유명한 랜드마크가 된다.	After that, the bridge becomes a famous around the world.

Review Test

A 빈칸에 어울리는 단어를 고르세요.

1. The Tower _____ on the Thames River is famous.
① Bring   ② Bread   ③ Brown   ④ Bridge

2. When the _____ rings, stand up and go outside.
① ball   ② belt   ③ bell   ④ bill

3. The stairs are quite _____. Watch out.
① sweet   ② steep   ③ strict   ④ several

4. It's not yours. It _____ to me.
① becomes   ② belongs   ③ beats   ④ behaves

5. I was _____ when I listened to the news.
① shocked   ② sharpened   ③ shown   ④ shared

6. The skirt is too _____ for me to wear. Give me a big one.
① large   ② dark   ③ long   ④ tight

7. Water boils at 100 _____ Celsius.
① deserts   ② desserts   ③ desires   ④ degrees

8. I have to make an _____ to study harder for the test.
① effort   ② erase   ③ effect   ④ exam

9. This statue is our city's _____.
① laugh   ② land   ③ landmark   ④ literature

10. He is my new _____ in my apartment.
① neighbor   ② near   ③ navigation   ④ navy

11. In the accident, the _____ saved my life.
① goal   ② guardian   ③ guard   ④ guardrail

12. Mind your _____, or you might fall down.
① style   ② step   ③ stress   ④ steam

13. The chair looks so expensive. It is made of _____.

    ① margin   ② marine   ③ market   ④ marble

14. The road is blocked because it's under _____.

    ① concert   ② concrete   ③ construction   ④ conclusion

15. The church is the most _____ place in the city.

    ① repeated   ② remarkable   ③ remind   ④ remember

16. _____ I am young, I can understand my mother.

    ① As soon as   ② After   ③ Even though   ④ Wherever

B 밑줄 친 단어와 비슷한 뜻을 가진 단어를 고르세요.

17. Put your bag <u>beside</u> the book on the table.

    ① across from   ② next   ③ under   ④ next to

18. Did you <u>finish</u> your homework?

    ① compete   ② complete   ③ complain   ④ compare

C 밑줄 친 단어와 반대되는 뜻을 가진 단어를 고르세요.

19. The economic situation is <u>unstable</u> nowadays.

    ① strong   ② stable   ③ steady   ④ steep

20. We should get up <u>early</u> in the morning.

    ① loosen   ② lack   ③ last   ④ late

Score: _____ /20

• Answers •

Unit 1 The Fortune   p.2

| Word Check |

Ⓐ 1. 해, 1년, 나이   2. 12개짜리 한 묶음, 다스
3. 주, 일주일   4. (풀을) 베다   5. 어린, 젊은
6. 고용하다   7. 손님, 고객   8. ~없이
9. 재산, 부, 행운   10. 코트, 경기장
11. 자선, 자선 단체   12. 담요   13. 집 없는
14. 아무것도 아닌 것   15. 배달
16. 아마, 어쩌면   17. 강도, 절도범   18. 초인종
19. 화나게 하다, 약 올리다   20. 연결하다
21. 심부름하다   22. 휴대 전화   23. 약한, 허약한
24. 망설이다, 주저하다
25. 덫, 함정, 계략; 덫으로 잡다, 가두다   26. 발명(품)
27. (돈을) 벌다, 얻다   28. 백만장자

Ⓑ 1. year   2. dozen   3. week   4. mowing
5. young   6. hired   7. customers   8. without
9. fortune   10. court   11. charity   12. blankets
13. homeless   14. Nothing   15. deliveries
16. Maybe   17. burglar   18. doorbell
19. make, angry   20. connects, doorbell
21. run, errands   22. doorbell, cell phone
23. weak   24. hesitates   25. trapped
26. invention   27. earns   28. millionaire

| Review Test |

Ⓐ 1. ②   2. ③   3. ③   4. ①   5. ②   6. ③   7. ④
8. ③   9. ②   10. ①   11. ②   12. ①   13. ④
14. ②

Ⓑ 15. ③   16. ②

Ⓒ 17. ②   18. ④   19. ①   20. ②

Unit 2 The Bat   p.6

| Word Check |

Ⓐ 1. 박쥐   2. 친한, 잘 아는, 익숙한   3. 포유동물
4. 펄럭이다, (날개를) 퍼덕이다
5. 걸다, 매달리다   6. 기르다   7. 먹이; 잡아먹다

8. 소리, 음; 소리를 내다, ~하게 들리다
9. 튀다, (소리가) 반사하다   10. 꽉 잡다, 움켜잡다
11. 죽음   12. 서쪽의   13. 그러나   14. 상징
15. 섬   16. 동굴   17. 해치다, 손상시키다   18. 천장
19. 매달리다   20. 거꾸로   21. 고요한, 차분한
22. 그림자   23. 외로운, 쓸쓸한
24. (호)주머니, 써야 할 돈; 포켓용의, 소형의
25. 마을   26. 쥐   27. 기념물, 기념비
28. 하늘을 나는 것, 비행사

Ⓑ 1. Bats   2. familiar   3. mammals   4. flap
5. hanging   6. raise   7. prey   8. sounds
9. bounce   10. grasp   11. death   12. Western
13. However   14. Bats, symbol   15. island
16. cave   17. harm   18. ceiling   19. dangling
20. upside down   21. calm   22. shadow
23. lonely   24. pocket   25. village   26. mice
27. memorial   28. Flier

| Review Test |

Ⓐ 1. ②   2. ③   3. ①   4. ②   5. ④   6. ③   7. ①
8. ③   9. ④   10. ④   11. ①   12. ②   13. ③
14. ③

Ⓑ 15. ④   16. ①   17. ②   18. ②

Ⓒ 19. ②   20. ①

Unit 3 Around the World   p.10

| Word Check |

Ⓐ 1. 과거의, 지나간; 과거   2. 전통   3. 나라, 시골
4. 받다   5. 대나무   6. 초읽기, 카운트다운
7. 달콤한; 단 것, 사탕 및 초콜릿류   8. 축제
9. 화려한, 공상적   10. 달력   11. 봉투
12. 교환하다; 교환   13. 폭죽
14. 매우 기쁘게 하다; 기쁨   15. 헐거운, 느슨한
16. 막 ~하려는 참이다   17. 흔들다, 움직이다; 몸부림
18. ~에서 나오다   19. ~에 넣다
20. 선물, 현재, 지금; 출석한, 참석한, 현재의
21. 까마귀   22. 베개   23. 소파, 긴 의자   24. 잠들다
25. 나타나다   26. 용서하다, 봐주다; 변명

27. 감싸다, 포장하다; 덮개, 포장지
28. 금의, 금으로 만든; 금

B 1. past   2. traditions   3. countries   4. receive
5. bamboo   6. countdown   7. sweet   8. festival
9. fancy   10. calendar   11. envelopes
12. exchange   13. firecrackers   14. delights
15. loose   16. is about to   17. wiggles
18. comes out of   19. put, in   20. present
21. crow   22. pillow   23. couch   24. falls asleep
25. shows up   26. Excuse   27. wraps   28. gold

| Review Test |

A 1. ②   2. ③   3. ④   4. ①   5. ②   6. ①   7. ④
8. ③   9. ①   10. ③   11. ②   12. ①   13. ③
14. ④

B 15. ②   16. ③   17. ③

C 18. ②   19. ④   20. ①

Unit **4** Life Cycle   p.14

| Word Check |

A 1. 싹트다, 싹트게 하다   2. 개구리
3. 양서류; 양서류의   4. (알을) 낳다, 놓다, 눕히다
5. ~으로 뒤덮이다   6. 부화하다, (알을) 깨다
7. 올챙이   8. 아가미   9. 폐, 허파
10. ~처럼 보이다, ~와 비슷하다   11. 새끼 개구리
12. 완전한, 완성한; 끝마치다   13. 다시, 한 번 더
14. 생활 주기   15. 행동하다, 처신하다
16. 믿을 수 없는   17. 나이, 시기, 시대
18. 못생긴, 추한   19. 피하다   20. ~할 때마다
21. 되돌아오다, 되돌리다   22. 왜, 어째서, ~한 이유
23. 알아보다, 인식하다   24. 새로운; 새로운 것
25. 설명하다   26. 사과하다
27. ~을 낮추어 보다, 업신여기다
28. 받아들이다, 인정하다, 수락하다

B 1. germinate   2. frog   3. amphibian   4. lays
5. are covered with   6. hatch   7. tadpole   8. gills
9. lungs   10. looks like, frog   11. froglet
12. frog, complete   13. again   14. life cycle
15. behaved   16. unbelievable   17. age
18. ugly   19. avoided   20. Whenever
21. turned back   22. why   23. recognize

24. new   25. explained   26. apologized
27. looked down on   28. accepted

| Review Test |

A 1. ②   2. ④   3. ①   4. ①   5. ②   6. ②   7. ④
8. ③   9. ①   10. ③   11. ③   12. ③   13. ②
14. ④   15. ④

B 16. ④   17. ①

C 18. ③   19. ②   20. ②

Unit **5** Space   p.18

| Word Check |

A 1. 우주선   2. 우주비행사   3. 달
4. 가까운; ~에서 가까이   5. 사건, 행사
6. 발사하다, 쏘다   7. 회전하다; 원
8. 경보기, 자명종; 놀라게 하다   9. 자료, 데이터
10. 다루다, 처리하다   11. 마침내, 최후로
12. (알갱이가) 미세한, 가는, 좋은; 벌금   13. 발자국
14. 역사   15. 우주, 공간   16. 외계인, 외국인, 이방인
17. 이상한, 기이한   18. 제안하다, 추천하다, 암시하다
19. 휴일, 축제일, 휴가   20. 토의하다, 토론하다
21. 우주복   22. 장비, 장치   23. 언덕, 낮은 산
24. 망원경   25. 위성, 인공위성   26. 화성
27. 부탁하다, 구걸하다   28. 접시

B 1. spacecraft   2. astronauts   3. moon   4. near
5. event   6. launched   7. circled   8. alarm
9. data   10. astronauts, dealt   11. finally
12. fine   13. footprints   14. history   15. space
16. aliens   17. weird   18. suggests
19. holiday, space   20. discuss   21. spacesuits
22. equipment   23. hill   24. telescope
25. satellite   26. Mars   27. beg   28. plate

| Review Test |

A 1. ①   2. ①   3. ④   4. ②   5. ③   6. ③   7. ②
8. ①   9. ④   10. ②   11. ③   12. ②   13. ③
14. ①

B 15. ②   16. ④   17. ③   18. ④

C 19. ③   20. ①

p.22

Unit 6 The Ocean

Word Check

A 1. 시내, 개울; 흐르다 2. 연어 3. 이주, 이동
4. 소금; 소금이 든, 소금 맛이 나는; 소금을 치다
5. ~에 들어가다, 입학하다 6. 어른; 어른의
7. 실패하다 8. 살아남다, 생존하다 9. 몇몇의
10. 되돌아가다, 돌려주다 11. 본능, 타고난 소질
12. 바위; 흔들다 13. 여성의, 암컷의; 여성, 암컷
14. 남성의, 수컷의; 남성, 수컷
15. 유람선 여행; 순항하다 16. 선장, 우두머리
17. 해적 18. 지역, 범위 19. 종종, 자주
20. 배 21. 끔찍한, 지독한
22. (방·마당 등을) 쓸다, 쓸어버리다
23. 차지하다, 인수하다 24. 위협하다, 협박하다
25. 승객, 여객 26. 보물, 보배
27. 찾다, 수색하다, 검색하다; 조사, 수색
28. 떨어져, 사라져

B 1. stream 2. salmon 3. migration 4. salt
5. enter 6. adult 7. fail 8. survive 9. several
10. return 11. instinct 12. rocks 13. Female
14. Male 15. cruise 16. captain 17. pirates
18. area 19. often 20. ship 21. terrible
22. ship, swept 23. take over 24. threaten
25. passengers 26. treasure 27. search
28. pirates, away

Review Test

A 1. ③ 2. ① 3. ② 4. ④ 5. ④ 6. ③ 7. ③
8. ④ 9. ① 10. ② 11. ④ 12. ① 13. ③
14. ① 15. ①

B 16. ② 17. ③ 18. ④

C 19. ② 20. ③

Unit 7 Great Adventures

p.26

Word Check

A 1. 북극의, 극지의 2. 탐험(대), 원정(대) 3. 성공하다
4. 시도하다; 시도 5. 해안, 물가 6. 준비하다
7. 탈것, 차 8. 영국인들 9. 기진맥진한
10. 고통을 겪다, 견디다 11. 동상; 동상을 입다
12. ~을 다 써버리다 13. 약간, 조금 14. 국가의
15. 극장 16. 삼각형 17. 딸 18. 이유
19. 영화, 화면 20. 잠수함 21. 소용돌이
22. ~에 끌어들이다 23. 거품; 거품이 나다
24. 악화되다 25. 상황, 처지
26. 누르다, 밀다, 강요하다; 언론
27. 세균, 박테리아 28. 영웅

B 1. polar 2. expeditions 3. succeeded
4. attempted 5. shore 6. prepared 7. vehicles
8. the English 9. exhausted 10. suffered
11. frostbite 12. ran out of 13. a few
14. national 15. theater 16. Triangle
17. daughter 18. reason 19. screen
20. submarine, expedition 21. whirlpool
22. submarine, drawn into 23. bubbles
24. getting worse 25. situation 26. presses
27. bacteria, bubbles 28. heroes

Review Test

A 1. ① 2. ② 3. ④ 4. ③ 5. ③ 6. ② 7. ①
8. ② 9. ④ 10. ③ 11. ① 12. ② 13. ④
14. ② 15. ①

B 16. ③ 17. ② 18. ③

C 19. ② 20. ④

Unit 8 The Honor

p.30

Word Check

A 1. 국제적인 2. 구석, 모퉁이
3. 존경하다, 영예를 주다; 명예, 영광 4. 물리학
5. 문학 6. 설립하다 7. ~으로 유명하다 8. 부, 재산
9. ~ 이래로, ~ 이후로 10. ~으로 이루어져 있다
11. 현금, 돈 12. 의식, 식 13. 기념일
14. ~보다 많은 15. 알다, 구별하다, 알고 지내다
16. 사전 17. 참가하다, 참여하다
18. 나아가다, 진보하다; 전진, 진보
19. 자신 있는, 확신에 찬 20. 경쟁, 대회
21. 모든 사람, 누구든지 22. 실수 23. 기회, 운
24. 질문, 문제; 질문하다 25. 부풀다, 더부룩하다
26. 방귀를 뀌다 27. 낄낄 웃다 28. 옳은, 정확한

B 1. international 2. corners 3. honors
4. physics 5. literature 6. established

7. is noted for   8. wealth   9. since   10. consists
11. cash   12. ceremonies   13. anniversary
14. More than   15. knows   16. dictionary
17. participates   18. advance   19. confident
20. competition   21. everybody   22. mistake
23. chance   24. question   25. bloated
26. breaks wind   27. giggle   28. correct

| Review Test |

Ⓐ 1. ④   2. ②   3. ④   4. ③   5. ③   6. ②   7. ④
8. ①   9. ③   10. ②   11. ④   12. ①   13. ④
14. ③   15. ②

Ⓑ 16. ①   17. ③   18. ①

Ⓒ 19. ②   20. ④

Unit ⑨ Step Back in Time   p.34

| Word Check |

Ⓐ 1. 가게; (물건을) 사다   2. 목욕, 욕조   3. 산
4. 분출하다, 폭발하다   5. 화산   6. 재, 화산재
7. 묻다   8. 재난   9. 나중에   10. 밝히다, 알아내다
11. 고고학자   12. 석화하다, 돌이 되다
13. 보존하다, 지키다   14. 남다, 여전히 ~이다
15. 시계   16. 가리키다; 뾰족한 끝
17. (기계 등을) 조정하다, 놓다, 두다; 한 벌, 한 세트
18. 돌다, 회전하다, 돌리다   19. 기절하다
20. 둘러싸다   21. 석기 시대   22. 도구   23. 날카로운
24. 끝, 가장자리   25. 칼
26. 궁금해하다, 놀라다; 놀라운   27. 날것의
28. 창조하다, 만들다

Ⓑ 1. shops   2. baths   3. mountain   4. erupted
5. volcano   6. ash   7. buried   8. disaster
9. later   10. uncovered   11. Archaeologists
12. petrified   13. preserved   14. remained
15. clock   16. points   17. set   18. spins
19. faints   20. surrounded   21. Stone Age
22. tools   23. sharp   24. edge   25. sharp, knife
26. wonder   27. raw   28. created

| Review Test |

Ⓐ 1. ②   2. ②   3. ④   4. ③   5. ②   6. ③   7. ①
8. ③   9. ④   10. ②   11. ①   12. ①   13. ④

14. ①   15. ③   16. ④

Ⓑ 17. ③   18. ②

Ⓒ 19. ④   20. ④

Unit ⑩ World Landmark   p.38

| Word Check |

Ⓐ 1. 종   2. 속하다   3. 대리석, 구슬   4. 수직의, 세로의
5. 건설   6. 기울다, 기대다   7. 불안정한
8. 노력   9. 중단하다, 그만두다   10. 기반, 기초
11. 끝내다   12. 정도, (온도·각도) 도, 학위
13. 비록 ~일지라도   14. 놀랄 만한, 뛰어난
15. 일찍   16. 이웃   17. 가파른, 경사가 급한
18. ~ 옆에, ~ 곁에   19. 다리   20. 밧줄
21. ~을 걸어서 건너다   22. 발을 헛디디다
23. 충격을 주다; 충격   24. 발걸음을 조심하다
25. 단단한, 꽉 조이는 곤란한; 단단히, 꽉
26. (계단) 난간, 가드레일   27. 방송 중에
28. 중요 지형지물, 명소, 랜드마크, 획기적 사건

Ⓑ 1. bell   2. belongs   3. marble   4. vertical
5. construction   6. lean   7. unstable   8. effort
9. ceased   10. foundation   11. finished
12. leans, degrees   13. Even though, leans
14. remarkable   15. early   16. neighbor
17. steep   18. beside   19. bridge   20. rope
21. walk across   22. misses his step
23. shocked   24. Mind your step   25. tight
26. guardrail   27. on air   28. landmark

| Review Test |

Ⓐ 1. ④   2. ③   3. ②   4. ②   5. ①   6. ④   7. ④
8. ①   9. ③   10. ①   11. ④   12. ②   13. ④
14. ③   15. ②   16. ③

Ⓑ 17. ④   18. ②

Ⓒ 19. ②   20. ④